Patrick Hoeveler

# CLASSIC WARBIRDS IN COLOR

## Musketeers of the Sky

**krause**

Published in North America, 2004 by

700 East State Street • Iola, WI 54990-0001
715-445-2214 • 888-457-2873
www.krause.com

Please call or write for our free catalog of publications. Our
toll-free number to place an order or obtain a free catalog is
(800) 258-0929.

Library of Congress Catalog Number: 2004100491
ISBN 0-87349-861-5

Printed in China by SNP Leefung

## Photographs

The colour pictures were taken by the author with
Nikon cameras and lenses; focal distances from 28 to
600mm. The historic photographs were provided by the
DEHLA collection and the author's private collection.

## About the author

Patrick Hoeveler has been fascinated by aeroplanes
since early childhood and has made his hobby his
career. Today, he is an editor for *Flug Revue*, Germany's
leading aviation and aerospace magazine. Amongst
other things, he is in charge of the magazine's 'aviation
history' section, and travels the globe to photograph
aeroplanes at numerous airshows.

# Contents

# Preface

People are always fascinated by these warbirds: the veterans of the past attract the visitors' attention at every airshow. The combination of the technical mastership of days past, and the breathtaking sound made by the military oldies, makes them the stars of any event – and the enthusiasm of the aviation fans is equalled by that of warbird operators and restorers. So despite increasing insurance premiums and high operating costs, the 'oldie' community is constantly being enriched by new projects.

Because these rare aeroplanes can cost millions of pounds in investment, at times the warbirds in this industry change hands frequently. Nevertheless, in spite of this changing situation, this book attempts to provide an overview of some selected historic aircraft that still exist today. The focus is on rare specimens from our own latitudes because unfortunately there would not have been enough room to list all the remaining veteran aircraft. But the positive outcome of having to be selective is that the most exciting stories of the chosen aircraft types have been recounted, whether they are set in the icy wildernesses of the polar regions or the jungles of exotic countries. Many projects, such as the rebuild of the Messerschmitt Me 262, seem to show that the attraction of classic aeroplanes is growing rather than diminishing. And this means that there is growing support for other, equally thrilling episodes.

I am particularly grateful to Adel Krämer and Marton Szigeti for their help with this book.

*Patrick Hoeveler*

February 2003, Bonn

# An early achievement

Everybody needs to learn the basics of their trade – but there may be exceptions to this rule. The legendary German aircraft designer Ernst Heinkel was only in his mid-twenties when, in 1913, he changed employers and left the Luft-Verkehrs-Gesellschaft LVG to join the Albatros-Flugzeugwerke, which had been founded in Berlin-Johannisthal in 1909. His first project for the new company was an instant success: he developed the two-seater biplane B I that could be flown in various configurations both as a military aeroplane as well as a trainer. The pilots were full of praise for Heinkel's creation, and acknowledged it as robust and reliable. In fact this reaction is not so surprising, given that this new aircraft

## ALBATROS B I

**Type:** Scout plane/trainer
**Crew:** 2
**Engine:** Mercedes D I
**Power:** 74kW (100hp)
**Length:** 8.57m
**Height:** 3.15m
**Wingspan:** 14.48m
**Empty weight:** 747kg
**Max take-off weight:** 1,080kg
**Max speed:** 105km/h
**Endurance:** Approx. 4 hours
**Armament:** None

featured a real novelty: although the spars and ribs of the wings were made of wood and covered with fabric, the young designer had used plywood to cover the entire fuselage, whereas most contemporary aircraft still had a fabric-covered fuselage. From 1914, a small number of B Is were used as trainers and scout planes. The follow-up version B II proved to be one of the most successful German two-seater trainers of its time. But Heinkel was an ambitious man and went on to found his own enterprise in Warnemünde in 1922.

The rebuilt aircraft is equipped with a 165hp Walter Minor VI from the Czech Republic.

The rebuilt Albatros B I (D-EKGH) has very forgiving flight characteristics and does not need a daredevil in the cockpit. This aeroplane was built by the Historic Aircraft Design Company (Historischer Flugzeugbau) in Fürstenwalde in 1999. The company had been encouraged to take on this project because of its previous success with the replica of an Etrich Taube. The Albatros made its debut at the International Aviation Exhibition (Internationale Luftfahrtausstellung) ILA in Berlin in 2002.

Busy times at the Albatros factory in Berlin: the B I and its successor, the B II, were amongst the aeroplanes with the highest production numbers in Germany at the time. There is only one original B I that has survived to the present day, and this can be admired in the Army History Museum (Heeresgeschichtliches Museum) in Vienna. In 1914, Albatros had developed the military biplane for the Austrian army.

# A random product becomes a legend

Twenty-one-year-old pilot Flight Lieutenant John Hopgood targets the wall of the Möhne dam in his Lancaster. However, the German anti-aircraft gunners have seen right through the intentions of the British and the bomber is badly hit by enemy fire. In spite of the critical situation, bomb aimer J.W. Fraser manages to drop the special bomb. But he is too late: the bomb bounces over the wall and remains ineffective. Hopgood is no longer able to hold the aircraft in the air and the 'Lanc' crashes. Fraser and the rear gunner Anthony Burcher are the only ones to survive the disaster. When the first bomber wave flies its fifth attack, the drop height and target distance form an exact match and the 'bouncing bomb', designed by bomb expert Barnes Wallis, destroys the dam. On the night of 16 to 17 May 1943, 1,600 people die in the flood waves. The Eder dam also collapses under the mighty attack of 617 Squadron of the Royal Air Force (RAF), a squadron that has carried the nickname 'Dam Busters' ever since. This mission made the Lancaster famous throughout Great Britain – yet it had been no more than a random product. The RAF had been looking for a new bomber and Avro had responded to the demand with its design of the two-engine Manchester. But due to its unreliable Vulture engines, this aircraft type proved to be a flop. Chief engineer Roy Chadwick demanded a proper engine and replaced the Vulture with the Merlin, which became one of the most, if not *the* most, famous British engine

## LANCASTER MK I

**Type:** Heavy bomber
**Crew:** 7
**Engines:** 4 Rolls-Royce Merlin 24
**Power:** 1,223kW (1,640hp) each
**Length:** 21.18m
**Height:** 6.10m
**Wingspan:** 31.09m
**Wing area:** 120.49m²
**Empty weight:** 16,738kg
**Max take-off weight:** 31,751kg
**Max speed:** 462km/h
**Range:** 4,072km
**Service ceiling:** 7,468m
**Armament:** Eight 7.7mm machine guns and a bomb load of up to 9,979kg

designs. Early tests showed that four of these engines were required for the new aircraft type. Chadwick modified the wings of the Manchester accordingly and the Avro 683 Lancaster was born. The prototype made its inaugural flight on 9 January 1941. It still featured a rather strange tail unit in three pieces. Soon afterwards, the middle fin was taken out. Altered and improved in this manner, the first series production aircraft was able to take off on 31 October 1941. To the surprise of its designers, the Lancaster far exceeded the performance data of its unlucky predecessor. Chadwick had unexpectedly managed to create the most successful British bomber ever.

*The only Lancaster that is still in active flying service in Europe is operated by the Battle of Britain Memorial Flight (BBMF) of the Royal Air Force. The Mk I PA474 was built by Vickers-Armstrong in Chester in mid-1945.*

## LONELY HEROES

Only a handful of more than 7,000 manufactured Lancasters have survived their service years, most of them in Canada. In that country alone, four complete Mk Xs can be found in museums and three additional aircraft are undergoing restoration. In the US, warbird collector Kermit Weeks from Florida is restoring the Mk X KB976. One Mk I is displayed in the Australian War Memorial in Canberra, one Mk VII is in the Royal Australian Air Force Museum in Perth, and another Mk VII stands in a museum in New Zealand. Europe, however, the original birthplace of the bomber, is a disappointing representative because apart from the Mk I R5868 in the Royal Air Force Museum in Hendon and the Mk X KB889 in the Imperial War Museum in Duxford, only the Lancaster Mk VII NX611 of the Lincolnshire Aviation Heritage Centre in East Kirby remains, able to taxi but not to fly. One other aircraft is currently being restored in France. Worldwide, only two Lancasters are fit to take to the air: the PA474 of the Battle of Britain Memorial Flight and the **Lancaster Mk X FM213 (C-GVRA)**. This 'Lanc' was built in Canada under licence and served in the Royal Canadian Air Force until 1964. After that, this precious flying machine was put up as a monument in Ontario, Canada. In 1977, the Canadian Warplane Heritage (CWH) in Mount Hope, Ontario, rescued the bomber from its sad existence and began the arduous task of restoring the Lancaster to an airworthy state. The aircraft had been exposed to the harsh Canadian climate, left out in the open for years, which added to its bad condition. But finally, on 11 September 1988, the FM213 was able to rise into the sky once more. In July 2002, it had a collision with the Douglas DC-3 of the CWH on the apron of Hamilton International Airport. Fortunately, the damage to the Lancaster was not too serious, and the 'oldie' has remained alive and kicking until today.

Right to the end of the 1990s, the memorial aircraft
displayed the markings of IX Squadron, which participated
in the attacks on the German battleship Tirpitz. The bomber
in the photograph was named Johnnie Walker.

The Lancaster PA474 of the RAF Memorial Flight Squadron had originally been destined for the Far East theatre, but the end of war in Asia called for a change of plan and the 'Lanc' was subsequently based with 82 Squadron in Africa as a reconnaissance plane. After that, the aircraft was meant to be converted into a drone but the RAF finally decided to hand it over to the Royal College of Aeronautics in Cranfield, where it was used for flight tests from 1954 to 1962.

*In action, the Lancaster proved to be an extremely reliable aircraft. At the time, it was recalled that on several occasions a particularly bold pilot used to fly rolls with the four-engine plane.*

When the career of the Lancaster PA474 as a test aircraft came to an end, the RAF decided to store the veteran for display in the planned museum at Hendon. Prior to this, the aircraft had played a role in the war films Operation Crossbow and The Guns of Navarone. However, destiny had other plans for this marvellous aircraft: at the time, 44 Squadron, the Lancaster's first combat unit, was flying another Avro product – the Vulcan, a jet-propelled delta-wing bomber – and this squadron was eager to take care of the historic treasure. The comprehensive restoration began in 1965. Finally, the PA474 joined the BBMF fleet and is currently based in Coningsby. The photograph shows one of the two Hurricanes of the BBMF escorting the Lancaster at the Royal International Air Tattoo 2002 at Fairford.

The Lancaster Mk I was equipped with the powerful Rolls-Royce Merlin engine. However, those aircraft that were powered by engines built by Packard under licence in the US were given the Avro designation Mk III.

In order to avoid a possible bottleneck in the production of Merlin engines, Avro fitted 300 units of the Lancaster Mk II with Hercules engines that were manufactured by Bristol. However, due to the production of the Packard engines, this redundancy policy soon proved to be unnecessary.

This Lancaster Mk I, on display in the Royal Air Force Museum, flew 137 missions during the war. It joined the Hendon exhibition in 1972.

This Lancaster Mk X has had its home in the Imperial War Museum in Duxford since 1986. The aircraft was built in Canada.

# The long road to the 'Flying Fortress'

Not often would the English Channel coast have looked so inviting. After a raid on Wilhelmshaven, Captain Robert Morgan literally dragged his damaged B-17F back to his base in Britain. The crew of the *Memphis Belle* are the first to accomplish 25 combat missions. 'If you'd like to know how we managed to fly through the hell of Europe and back 25 times, I give you one word: teamwork!' Morgan and his men made a tour through the US in 1943, and this kind of talk enthused troops and the population alike. The *Memphis Belle* became a cult object, and the film of the same name increased its reputation even more. From then onwards, the Boeing B-17 became a symbol for the mighty power of the US Army Air Force. However, it hadn't always been like that, and things looked very different in the early days of the aircraft's history. During the 1930s, the US Air Force was regarded as simply outdated in comparison to the air forces of Europe and Japan, and it was only the start of the war in Europe that made the American generals realise the truth of the matter. The attack on Pearl Harbor was a huge shock for the US and initiated an unprecedented American armament effort. As early as August 1934, the Defence Department had demanded a 350km/h bomber with a range of 3,200 kilometres. In response, Boeing produced its model 299, which looked like a promising design. The four-engine monoplane with low-set wings was a full-metal construction, and made its maiden flight on 28 July 1935. But tragically, the aircraft crashed several months later on a test flight. Due to its enormous preinvestment, the company came close to bankruptcy. It was rescued just in time by an order for 13 pre-series YB-17 aircraft in January 1936. Finally, on 20 October 1939, the US Army Air Corps was able to receive its first B-17B from the series production. The follow-up version B-17C was also used by the Royal Air Force but displayed obvious deficiencies with regard to its defensive armament as well as its armour plating during operation. The designers returned to their drawing boards and created the B-17E. This bomber looked like a nearly new aircraft: it featured a new rudder that had been extended in flight direction, and additional machine-gun turrets. From October 1943, the B-17G was introduced to the combat units. This model had the highest production numbers. It was equipped with a chin turret, which increased the number of machine guns aboard to twelve and truly justified the aircraft's nickname 'Flying Fortress'. Towards the end of the war, new and more powerful versions replaced the loyal 'Fort'. The last of a total of 12,731 'Flying Fortresses' was delivered by Boeing on 13 April 1945.

## B-17G FLYING FORTRESS

**Type:** Heavy bomber
**Crew:** 10
**Engines:** 4 Wright Cyclone R-1820-97
**Power:** 1,014kW (1,380hp) each
**Length:** 22.66m
**Height:** 5.85m
**Wingspan:** 31.63m
**Wing area:** 132.00m²
**Empty weight:** 14,822kg
**Max take-off weight:** 32,616kg
**Max speed:** 484km/h
**Range:** 3,219km
**Service ceiling:** 10,860m
**Armament:** Twelve 12.7mm machine guns and a bomb load of up to 4,350kg

*Returning to base: the Duxford-based B-17G 44-85784 (G-BEDF) comes in to land after a test flight. The Sally B is owned by the company B-17 Preservation Limited. It was built under licence by Lockheed-Vega and was used as a test aircraft and weather observation aircraft until 1954, when it was transferred to the French National Geographic Institute (Institut Géographique National). In 1975, the aircraft came to Britain and has been shown as Sally B at many airshows since. In order to finance the high operating costs, a club was founded in 1980 so that its supporters could contribute to the warbird's preservation, which meant it did not have to be sold to the US.*

## FORTRESS SQUADRON

More than 40 complete Flying Fortresses have survived to the present day, 14 of which are still in flying condition. The majority are based in the US. One example is the **B-17G 44-8543 (N3701G) Chuckie**, the star of the Vintage Flying Museum in Fort Worth, Texas. In spite of its rather unusual name, the **B-17G 44-83563 (N9563G) Fuddy Duddy** is the pride of the National Warplane Museum in Genesco in the US state of New York. The **B-17G 44-85778 (N3509G) Miss Angela** is now a part of the Palm Springs Air Museum collection in California.

Two of the static display B-17s are located in Brazil. There is one specimen in store in the Aviation Museum (Musée de l'Air) in Le Bourget, and two more aircraft can be admired, one in the Imperial War Museum in Duxford and the other in the RAF Museum in Hendon. The only remaining aircraft of the earlier versions is the B-17D The Swoose, currently stored in Silver Hill, Maryland.

Above: The Thunderbird takes off for a flight display at Oshkosh. The B-17G 44-85718 (N900RW) originally came from France and has been flying for the Lone Star Flight Museum in Galveston since 1987. This is another aircraft from the fleet of the French National Geographic Institute (Institut Géographique National), but after a brief stay in Duxford, where the aircraft was registered as G-FORT, it found its way to Texas.

Right: Oshkosh 1995. The Flying Fortress owned by Evergreen awaits its next flight display. Today, the B-17G 44-83785 (N207EV) can be found next to Howard Hughes' famous Spruce Goose in the Evergreen Aviation Museum in McMinnville, Oregon. The trademark of the B-17G, which is the version of the bomber with the highest production numbers, is its chin machine-gun turret.

*Above: This is not the real Memphis Belle but the star of the film with the same name. The B-17G 44-83546 (N3703G) was used as a fire-fighting aircraft until David Tallichet of the Military Aircraft Restauration Corporation restored it to its original state. The original Memphis Belle, ie the war aircraft, can be admired in Memphis, Tennessee, where it has been on display since 1946. At present it is kept in the Mud Island Museum of the Memphis Belle Memorial Association.*

One of the two remaining flying 'Forts' in Europe is the B-17G 44-8846 (F-AZDX) Pink Lady, based in Orly, France. The bomber was built under licence by Lockheed-Vega in Burbank and delivered to the US Army Air Force on 13 January 1945. After its active service with the USAF (its last base was Olmstead AFB until 10 November 1954), it came to the French National Geographic Institute (Institut Géographique National), where it was used for cartography purposes; it operated from Creil airfield from 1954 onwards. In 1985 the aircraft was taken on by the organisation Still Flying Fortress (Organisation Forteresse Toujours Volante) in cooperation with the Association Jean-Baptiste Salis. In the film Memphis Belle, the aircraft flew as Mother and Country.

Bob Collings restored the Nine-O-Nine from a former water bomber. Today, the B-17G 44-83575 (N93012) and the B-24 Liberator are the flagships of the Collings Foundation in Stow.

The Flying Fortress was heavily armed, and flying in large formations the bomber was not to be underestimated by enemy fighters.

After more than ten years of workshop overhaul, the Aluminium Overcast of the Experimental Aircraft Association is flying once more in the colours of the 398th Bomb Group. On 18 May 1945, the B-17G 44-85740 (N5017) entered service with the US Army Air Force, but after only a couple of years it was sold to a private company for 750 dollars. Since then the aircraft was used as a transport plane and an agricultural spraying aircraft. In February 1978, William Harrison from Oklahoma and a group of investors bought the former bomber with the aim of restoring it to its original state. However, the operating costs of such a large warbird are exorbitant, and in 1983 the group decided to donate the aircraft to the EAA, which restored it in great detail, refitting all the former military equipment.

Workplace of a Fortress pilot: the cockpit of the B-17G from the Planes of Fame Museum in Ohio. The Piccadilly Lady is currently being brought back into an airworthy state.

*The Royal Air Force operated several early Fortresses with the old tail unit. One of the reasons why the RAF rejected the bomber was that it had insufficient defensive armament.*

The only flying representative of the F series has been loyal to its manufacturer to the present day: the B-17F 42-29782 (N17W) Boeing Bee belongs to the Museum of Flight in Seattle and has been restored with great effort by Boeing. After its decommissioning in 1946, the bomber was put up as a war memorial in Stuttgart, Arkansas, for seven years. Then it underwent a major overhaul and was used as a spraying aircraft and water bomber. During its long career, the aircraft also participated in the films Tora Tora Tora and Memphis Belle.

The B-17G Mary Alice stands in the American Air Museum of the Imperial War Museum in Duxford. In the 1940s, the aircraft was operated as a civilian transport plane until finally it ended up in the French National Geographic Institute.

*Above right: a highlight – even at the gigantic Oshkosh flight meeting. The EAA's Aluminium Overcast flies side by side with the B-17G 44-83872 (N7227C) Texas Raiders of the Commemorative Air Force. The Aluminium Overcast has also belonged to the CAF in Midland, Texas, since 1967. Before that and until 1955, the bomber had been operated by the US Navy as a patrol aircraft with the designation PB-1W. Then it was flown by a private company and used for cartography purposes. Another B-17G, 44-83514 (N9332Z) Sentimental Journey, is also part of the CAF. This aircraft is based in Mesa, Arizona. After a career as a water bomber, it joined the CAF in 1978.*

*The B-17G 44-85829 (N3193G) Yankee Lady was restored with great attention to detail in 1986 by the Yankee Air Museum in Willow Run, Michigan. Right up to the end of the 1950s, the aircraft flew as a rescue plane for the US Coast Guard. After that, like many other Fortresses, it was used for air photography missions as well as fire fighting and pest control. It also played its part in the film Tora Tora Tora.*

# Pacemaker

The US Air Force ordered 250 units of Boeing's newest bomber project straight from the drawing board. A study group that included the aviation pioneer Charles Lindbergh had been able to convince the US Army Air Corps that a so-called super bomber, with a speed of 640km/h and a range of 8,600km, was a necessary addition to the fleet. Considering all the technical challenges, the military played a risky game when ordering this aircraft. The B-29 was twice the weight of the B-17 and was regarded as the world's heaviest aircraft, and the high wing loading posed serious problems for the designers. Chief aerodynamics engineer George Schairer came up with a solution for the problem: he created a new wing profile. Never before had spars of such dimensions been produced for a series production aircraft: but even the enormous Wright R-3350 engine with its 18 cylinders and 1,617kW (2,200hp) could not provide the required airspeed. The only remaining option was to reduce the drag. In addition, it proved impossible for gunners to operate the machine-gun posts (as in the B-17) at such great cruise heights. Again, the Boeing team found a revolutionary answer to this challenge: remote-controlled gun turrets. The gunners were positioned in five sighting stations behind glass domes in the pressurised fuselage, from where they operated the fire control system.

The B-29 had its great day on 21 September 1942: the first prototype took off for its maiden flight from the Boeing airfield in Seattle. However, the programme suffered a serious setback when due to an engine fire, the second B-29 crashed into a meat packaging plant near Seattle. But the US Air Force could not wait any longer for the bomber and had to make its production its main priority. In greatest secrecy, the first few aircraft were moved to India via North Africa. From there, the bombers needed to cross the Himalayas in order to transport fuel and weapons to the advanced bases in China. To fly one combat mission, it was necessary to make seven logistics flights via the 'Hump'. With the conquest of the Pacific islands, the B-29 bases could get closer to the Japanese mainland, although the missions still took up to 15 hours flight time. But in spite of repeated mass attacks with firebombs, the Japanese government kept up its resistance, and because of this, US President Harry Truman authorised the use of the atomic bomb. At 9.15am on 6 August 1945, the crew of the *Enola Gay* dropped its ordnance, the so-called 'Little Boy'. The second mission followed on 8 August with

Every member of the Commemorative Air Force has the rank of a colonel. At present, the organisation has about 11,000 members from the age of 18 to 100.

Operating *Fifi* is only made possible through the efforts of a team of highly motivated volunteers. The Superfortress is regarded as the most complicated aircraft in the Texas-based warbird fleet.

## B-29 SUPERFORTRESS

**Type:** Strategic bomber
**Crew:** 10
**Engines:** 4 Wright R-3350-29
**Power:** 1,617kW (2,200hp) each
**Length:** 30.18m
**Height:** 9.02m
**Wingspan:** 43.05m
**Wing area:** 161.27m²
**Empty weight:** 34,020kg
**Max take-off weight:** 62,560kg
**Max speed:** 575km/h
**Range:** 5,150km
**Service ceiling:** 10,240m
**Armament:** Twelve 12.7mm machine guns in turrets, one 20mm cannon in the tail, and a bomb load of up to 9,072kg

Watch out: Superfortress! The B-29 Fifi of the Commemorative Air Force is the star at all warbird demonstrations. The bomber's imposing effect is made all the more dramatic by an ample use of pyrotechnics. The photograph shows the reflection of a huge wall of flames on the underside of the fuselage.

*Bock's Car*'s raid on Nagasaki. Initially in the post-war period, and also later in Korea, the Superfortress continued to be used as a bomber. After that it operated in various support roles. The Superfortress was decommissioned as late as 21 June 1960.

### LONELY WARBIRD

The B-29A 44-62070 (N529B) Fifi of the Commemorative Air Force is the last remaining airworthy Superfortress worldwide. The star of the Commemorative Air Force (CAF) can boast a colourful history. On 31 July 1945, the bomber was commissioned by the US Army Air Force in Salinas, Kansas. Later on, the aircraft was used as a trainer. In January 1948 it was decided to park the B-29 in the desert. However, as the Korean War gathered impetus, the USAF took it out of storage and recommissioned it to bomber standard. After a period of active service with 310th Bombardment Wing, the Air Force modified the B-29A into a TB-29A trainer. In October 1956, the aircraft was finally taken out of service. Once a proud aeroplane, it ended up on a US Navy firing range in China Lake in the middle of the Californian desert. That would have nearly been it, if it hadn't been for a lucky accident. The CAF (at the time it was still called Confederate Air Force) had been on the lookout for a B-29 warbird for quite a while, when it got a tip from a pilot who claimed to have spotted several Superfortresses on a flight over China Lake in 1971. The existence of these aircraft came as a surprise, given that the USAF didn't officially have any of these bombers in their inventories. It took many difficult negotiations with the Air Force and Navy, but finally a team of 'oldie' enthusiasts was allowed to choose a Superfortress and make it ready for the ferry flight to the CAF headquarters, which were then in Harlingen, Texas – all within a period of three weeks. It must have been a miracle that Fifi survived the six-hour flight to its new home without any problems. In Texas the aircraft underwent a major overhaul. Today the former giant is based in Midland.

There are some thirty other B-29s worldwide: one exists in South Korea, another is in the Imperial War Museum in Duxford and a further 24 aircraft can be found in the US. One other restoration project failed in 1995: Darryl Greenamyer brought the Kee Bird, which had made an emergency landing in Greenland in 1947, back into an airworthy state. However, the bomber caught fire during take-off, the devastated crew having a near escape. The B-29 Doc is currently being restored by volunteers in the Boeing plant in Wichita, and the aircraft is scheduled for its second maiden flight in 2003. The two bombers that dropped the atom bomb are also still around: Bock's Car is in the USAF Museum in Dayton, while Enola Gay is supposed to be presented to the public after extensive restoration works in the Udvar Hazy Center of the National Air and Space Museum at the Washington Dulles airport in late 2003.

US ARMY B-29A
ARMY AIR FORCES SER NO 44-62C

ENOLA GAY
THE RIGHT STUFF
THE AMERICAN WAY
FAT MAN, LITTLE BOY
ROSWELL

*The Superfortress owes its power to its extremely low-drag aerodynamic design. The aircraft was far ahead of its time. The Soviet Union even made a copy of a B-29 when a US aircraft had to make an emergency landing on USSR territory. The copied aircraft went into series production at Tupolew's plants and was designated Tu-4.*

It was Bock's Car that dropped the atom bomb on Nagasaki. Today, the aircraft is in the US Air Force Museum in Dayton, Ohio.

Below: A B-29 starts its engines on its Saipan base on the Marshall Islands for the next mission over Japan.

The only Superfortress that remains in Europe has been secured by the Imperial War Museum in Duxford.

# A bomber outruns the fighters

Surprisingly, the first modern monoplane of the Royal Air Force (RAF) was not a fighter plane. It was a two-engine bomber, and it introduced the new era of British aircraft construction. The Bristol Blenheim was developed in 1936. The aircraft had a retractable gear, controllable pitch prop and flaps, and was much faster than the slower, fixed-gear biplanes such as the Gloster Gladiator. The development of the aircraft had originally started with an eight-seater passenger plane for Lord Harold Rothmere, owner of a newspaper empire that included the *Daily Mail*. However, when the aircraft displayed its maximum speed of 480km/h, the RAF became increasingly interested in the new project. The Air Ministry reacted quickly, and soon set up specifications for a medium bomber, in August 1935. Only a month later, the Air Ministry ordered 150 aircraft with the designation Blenheim I. In contrast to the civilian Type 142, the designers moved the wing upwards to the middle of the fuselage in order to create space for the bomb shaft. The Blenheim was also fitted with a shortened glass nose. After its inaugural flight on 25 June 1936, the 'speed wonder' continued to fulfil all expectations, and the squadrons received their aircraft from March 1937. Bristol manufactured a total of 1,552 Mk Is, which were also used by Finland, Yugoslavia, Romania and Turkey. Production of these was stopped in late 1938 and the old model was replaced by the Mk IV, designed in response to a demand for a new bomber for coastguard purposes. In autumn 1939, the first new aircraft arrived at their bases, and could be easily recognised by their lengthened nose. Apart from the 1,930 aeroplanes that were produced in Britain, numerous other aircraft were built in Canada under the name of Bolingbroke. However, these aircraft stemmed from an era of rapid design changes, and it soon became clear that the Blenheim had become outdated by other models. In comparison to modern fighters such as the Messerschmitt Bf 109 or the Mitsubishi Zero, the Blenheim didn't stand a chance. Its designers had wholly focused on its speed, and to its long-term detriment, had rather neglected its defensive armament and armour-plating.

## BLENHEIM MK IV

**Type:** Medium bomber
**Crew:** 3
**Engines:** 2 Bristol Mercury XV
**Power:** 686kW (933hp) each
**Length:** 12.98m
**Height:** 3.00m
**Wingspan:** 17.17m
**Wing area:** 43.6m²
**Empty weight:** 4,435kg
**Max take-off weight:** 6,523kg
**Max speed:** 428km/h
**Range:** 2,531km
**Service ceiling:** 8,310m
**Armament:** One machine gun in the wing and two in the turret (all 12.7mm) as well as a bomb load of up to 454kg

The only remaining flying Blenheim worldwide is operated by the Aircraft Restauration Company in Duxford. In May 1943, the aircraft was taken over by the Royal Canadian Air Force as a Bolingbroke with the serial number 10201. Three years later, after its decommissioning, it was put into store in Manitoba by its new private owner. In 1984, the bomber ended up as a restoration project with the Strathallan Collection in Scotland. However, work on the aircraft really only gathered momentum when Graham Warner of the Aircraft Restauration Company acquired it in 1989.

Shortly before its second inaugural flight on 18 May 1993, 50 years to the day after its initial delivery to a combat squadron, the Blenheim G-BPIV got its black camouflage paint – essential for its role as a night fighter of 68 Squadron. Owner Graham Warner's persistence paid off: while his first Blenheim, restored over a period of twelve years, crashed only one month after its inaugural flight, this second aircraft became a most rewarding 'oldie'.

*Originally, the aircraft had entered service as a Bolingbroke in 1943, but today it flies with the August 1940 markings of a Blenheim Mk IV of 82 Squadron.*

In spite of its enhanced defensive armament, the Blenheim Mk IV was unable to defend itself against the modern enemy fighters. Nevertheless, a Blenheim Mk IV of 139 Squadron flew the RAF's first World War II mission over Germany: a reconnaissance flight over Wilhelmshaven. From mid-1942, the Blenheim was replaced by the de Havilland Mosquito.

In contrast to the Blenheim Mk I, the Mk IV series features a lengthened nose. No representative of the first version of the bomber, which was also used as a heavy bomber, has survived until the present day. Nearly all of the Blenheims that still exist today were built in Canada and are really Bolingbrokes; therefore, most exhibited complete aircraft are found in Canadian museums. Even the bomber on display in the RAF Museum in Hendon is really a Bolingbroke of the Royal Canadian Air Force (RCAF). Another aircraft of this type can be admired in the Army Museum in Brussels, and one Bristol Mk IV is in store in the Finnish Air Force Museum in Tikkakoski.

# A durable oldie

It is the year 1932. The sun burns down on the Iraqi desert. A biplane takes off for a patrol flight over the British province. Only a few months later, in far-away Europe, modern and fast cruise aircraft such as the Heinkel He 70, with a speed of more than 300km/h, will propel aircraft construction into a new era. However, this biplane flying over the Persian Gulf in 1932 was designed during World War I. It is a Bristol Fighter – regarded as one of the most successful fighter aircraft of its time and legendary for its durability. The two-seater fighter aircraft made its inaugural flight on 9 June 1916 and got off to a bad start. No. 48 Squadron of the Royal Flying Corps (RFC) was flying the early F.2A version of the airplane and was using the wrong tactics. The pilots were instructed to focus on getting their back-seated observers/gunners into a suitable position to direct their backwards-firing machine guns against the enemy. This manoeuvre was bound to fail – during the very first mission the British suffered heavy losses, with two of their aircraft being shot down by Manfred von Richthofen, the 'Red Baron', alone. The British pilots had to learn their lessons quickly, and changed tactics. They started to use their Fighters like single-seater aircraft while their observers protected the vulnerable tail area. In May 1917 the improved F.2B version led to a breakthrough. Due to its bigger fuel tank and ammunition stores as well as a more powerful engine, the Bristol aircraft became a very big seller. By the time production stopped in 1926 the British had built nearly 4,500 Bristol Fighters. The Fighter remained in active service in New Zealand until 1938, demonstrating its superb performance in one of the fastest-developing eras of aviation history.

## FIGHTER F.2B

**Type:** Fighter
**Crew:** 2
**Engine:** 1 Rolls-Royce Falcon III
**Power:** 205kW (279hp)
**Length:** 7.87m
**Height:** 2.97m
**Wingspan:** 11.96m
**Wing area:** 37.71m²
**Empty weight:** 790kg
**Max take-off weight:** 1,173kg
**Max speed:** 201km/h
**Endurance:** 3 hours
**Service ceiling:** 6,553m
**Armament:** One forward-firing machine gun and one machine gun on a Scarff ring, operated by the observer/gunner

*Living history: after landing in Old Warren, the 85-year-old Bristol Fighter taxis to its shutdown position. After a major overhaul by Bristol, the F.2B D8096 (G-AEPH) was ready to take to the skies again in February 1952. Since then, the 'oldie' has enjoyed an active flying career, only briefly interrupted from 1980 to 1982. A second aircraft is currently being restored.*

The D8096 was built in 1918 but did not take part in
World War I. The aircraft was operated by No. 208
Squadron in 1923 in Turkey.

The original design of the Fighter responded to the demand for an artillery scout plane. However, even before the first specimen with the designation R.2A was ready to fly, its designers had already recognised the aircraft's potential as a fighter plane and renamed it F.2A. Today, there are no aeroplanes of this version left. The photograph shows an original F.2B, which can be seen in the Imperial War Museum in Duxford, whereas the Fighter in the RAF Museum in Hendon has been composed of parts from several aircraft. There is one other aircraft still flying worldwide: it is owned by the Fighter Collection in Duxford. It consists in parts of components from an F.2B from 1918 and its fuselage had come from Weston-on-the-Green because in Weston a farmer had built a barn from parts of a Fighter's fuselage structure. The second 'inaugural flight' of the F.2B D8084 (G-ACAA) took place on 30 June 1998. Unfortunately, the aircraft subsequently suffered from engine problems and had to be grounded for a while. The Army Museum in Brussels also owns a Fighter from Weston. There are also some rebuilds with limited airworthiness in existence.

The Fighter owed its success in parts to the unconventional way in which its wings were mounted to the fuselage. The designers moved the wings downwards and fixed them some distance below the fuselage. This wing arrangement allowed the crew to have a better view.

# A liberator in the shadow

This is what hell might look like: more than 230 anti-aircraft batteries fire incessantly, setting the night sky over Romania alight. Thick smoke covers the gigantic oil refineries of Ploesti. German fighters roar high above the plants that have become vital for the German Reich's survival. Right in the middle of this spectacular chaos 161 American bombers are flying at an extremely low level without a fighter escort: 52 of them will never return. The first mass attack of the Consolidated B-24 Liberator on 1 August 1943 made history as one of the most risky and heavily loss-making missions of WWII. Although this attack was not the only one of its kind, public awareness of the Liberator is still not as high as that of the B-17 Flying Fortress – this despite the fact that the Liberator, with more than 18,000 aircraft built, is the US warplane with the highest ever production numbers. In January 1939, the new Commander of the US Air Force, General Henry Arnold, had asked Consolidated to design a new long-range bomber that was superior to the B-17. As a result, the designers came up with a concept for the US Army Air Force that was centred around the aircraft range as the main priority. Their efforts were rewarded when, on 30 March 1939, Consolidated was commissioned to build a prototype with the designation XB-24. Designers and engineers exceeded all expectations. The XB-24 was constructed in record time, and as early as on 29 December 1939, the aircraft took off from San Diego for its inaugural flight. Later on, the series aircraft did indeed achieve greater ranges than the B-17. However, they were slower and more difficult to fly than their competitor, and because of this, as from November 1943, the US Army Air Force used this aircraft type mainly in the Pacific theatre. With the end of the war the working days of the B-24 also came to an end. Now, modern bombers such as the B-29 Superfortress have become the standard equipment of the Air Force, and nearly all Liberators have been melted down. Only the Indian Air Force flew the US industries' manufacturing wonder up to the 1960s.

## B-24J LIBERATOR

**Type:** Heavy bomber
**Crew:** 10
**Engines:** 4 Pratt & Whitney R-1830-65 Twin Wasp
**Power:** 895kW (1,200hp) each
**Length:** 20.47m
**Height:** 5.49m
**Wingspan:** 33.53m
**Wing area:** 37.36m²
**Empty weight:** 16,555kg
**Max take-off weight:** 32,296kg
**Max speed:** 467km/h
**Range:** 3,380km
**Service ceiling:** 8,535m
**Armament:** Ten 12.7mm machine guns and a bomb load of up to 5,806kg

The only remaining piece: the B-24 (N224) of the Collins Foundation is the only airworthy J-version and the second of two remaining active Liberators worldwide. The restoration of the rare bomber took more than 97,000 man hours. The 44-44052 was built in Fort Worth in August 1944 and was delivered to the Royal Air Force, which used it in the Pacific region. After that, the aircraft was acquired by the Indian Air Force, who kept the ageing fighter flying up to the 1960s. Finally, aircraft collector Doug Arnold of the company Warbirds of Britain brought the B-24 to Britain in 1981. Three years later, Richard Collings bought the rare bomber. Collings had the Liberator restored by experts in Kissimee, Florida. The inaugural Flight of the 'All American' was on 8 August 1989.

In the meantime, the Liberator has been flying as Golden Girl, here to be seen on Nellis Air Force Base. With 6,678 units built, the B-24J became the version of the bomber with the highest production numbers. A contributing factor for the achievement of such high figures by Consolidated was a huge purpose-built 1,220x100m manufacturing hangar in Fort Worth, Texas.

Due to its spacious fuselage, the B-24 could be used in various roles – as a bomber, a transport plane, a tanker and also a marine patrol aircraft.

The world's oldest Liberator flies for the Commemorative Air Force in Texas. Originally, the aircraft with the registration AM927 and the designation LB-30 (Liberator British) was to be delivered to the Royal Air Force in 1941, but it crashed on the ferry flight in Canada. The manufacturer repaired the bomber and used it as a transport plane during the war. Later on, Consolidated sold the Liberator to a can manufacturer as a business plane. From there, the veteran came to the national Mexican oil company PEMEX and was finally bought by the Confederate Air Force in 1967. Since then, the Diamond Lil (N24927), in the colours of the 98th Bomb Group, has had a great deal of admiration.

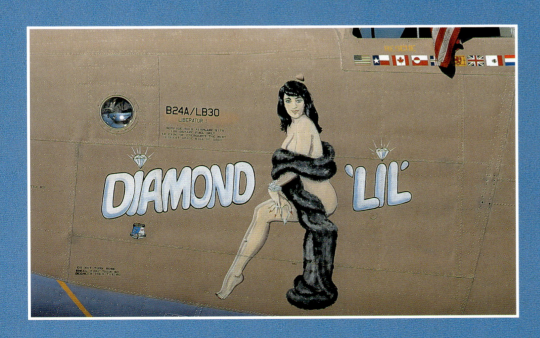

Diamond Lil was the twenty-fifth aircraft to leave the production lines at Consolidated.

Similar to the Flying Fortress, the Liberator also had heavy defensive armament (the photograph shows the gunners in the rear fuselage of a B-24N).

Below: This B-24L had been in Indian service; it came to Great Britain in 1974 and is now displayed in the RAF Museum in Cosford. The Imperial War Museum in Duxford is also currently restoring a Liberator. Today, a total of eleven complete aircraft exist. In the US, one B-24 each can be found in the USAF Museum in Dayton, the Castle Air Museum, Kalamazoo Air Zoo, Pima Air and Space Museum as well as on Barksdale AFB. The Canadian National Aviation Museum in Ottawa and the museum of the Indian Air Force in Palam also own one each of these rare aircraft. In addition, a few PB4Y Privateer Navy versions with a single-piece tail unit are still being flown as water bombers, although a recent crash has thrown their airworthiness into considerable uncertainty.

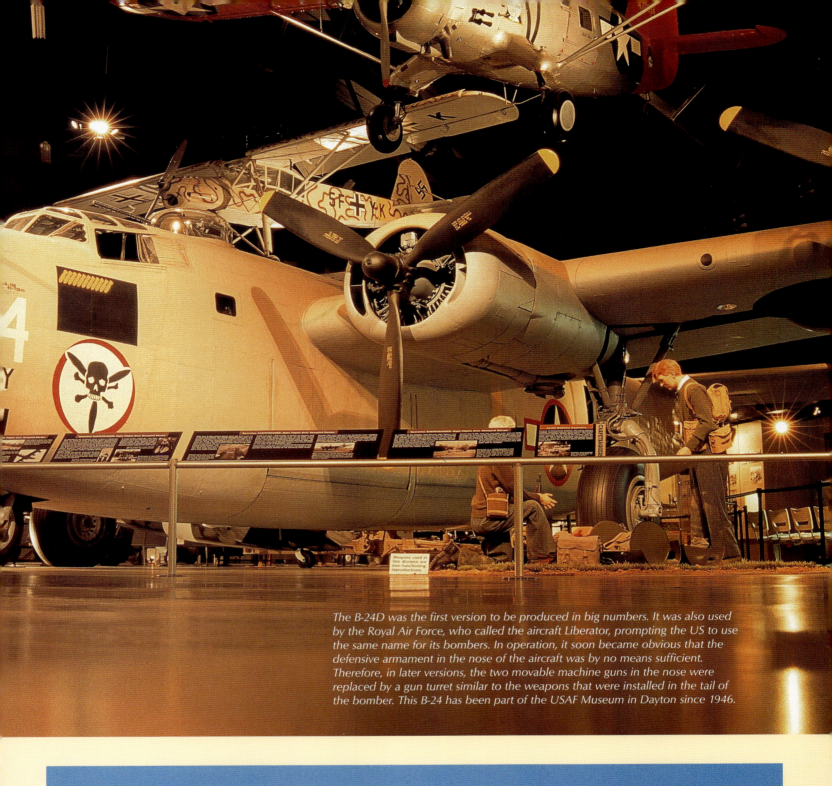

The B-24D was the first version to be produced in big numbers. It was also used by the Royal Air Force, who called the aircraft Liberator, prompting the US to use the same name for its bombers. In operation, it soon became obvious that the defensive armament in the nose of the aircraft was by no means sufficient. Therefore, in later versions, the two movable machine guns in the nose were replaced by a gun turret similar to the weapons that were installed in the tail of the bomber. This B-24 has been part of the USAF Museum in Dayton since 1946.

Thanks to the new Davis wing profile, the designers were able to use a much thinner wing.

# A short career

The beginnings of de Havilland's ultimate fighter plane didn't look particularly promising. In a competition for a new all-weather fighter for the Royal Air Force in 1951, the test aircraft DH 110 succumbed to its rival, the later Gloster Javelin. But unexpected help was offered by the Royal Navy in 1952 as they were looking for a suitable aircraft for their carrier fleet. After the DH 110 had proved its seaworthiness, the Navy gave the go-ahead for the airplane with the double tail boom, a de Havilland trademark. The arrangement of the crew was a novelty. The designers moved the pilot's cockpit to the right and placed the navigator in a compartment next to the pilot. The inaugural flight of the first British fighter exclusively armed with guided missiles finally took place on 20 March 1957. The Sea Vixen FAW 1 was delivered to the first combat squadron in July 1959. From 1964, the first version was replaced by the FAW 2 with its additional fuel tanks. But the Navy's decision to get rid of aircraft carriers with conventional aircraft brought the Sea Vixen's career to a premature end. In January 1972, the remainder of a total of 148 carrier aircraft was decommissioned by 899 Squadron, the Sea Vixen's last combat unit.

The Sea Vixen FAW 2 with the registration XS576 has found a new home in the Imperial War Museum. The aircraft really belongs to the Old Flying Machine Company. A total of twelve aircraft is still in existence, all of which are based in Britain.

## SEA VIXEN FAW 2

**Type:** Carrier-based all-weather fighter
**Crew:** 2
**Engines:** 2 Rolls-Royce Avon 208
**Power:** 49.9kN each
**Length:** 16.94m
**Height:** 3.27m
**Wingspan:** 15.24m
**Wing area:** 60.20m²
**Empty weight:** 14,367kg
**Max take-off weight:** 20,702kg
**Max speed:** 1,030km/h
**Range:** 3,200km
**Service ceiling:** 14,640m
**Armament:** Four Red Top missiles and various other external loads

The only remaining flying Sea Vixen in the world can boast a colourful history. The Royal Navy received the XP924 as an all-weather fighter FAW 2 in 1964 and operated it with 899 Squadron. In 1973, the carrier aircraft finally came to the Royal Aircraft Establishment, a British research facility, where it was converted into a drone and was given the designation D 3. From 1986 to 1991, the Sea Vixen flew in this new role from Llanbedr. During the following years it remained grounded until Gwyn Jones bought the aircraft in 1996. In order to operate the Sea Vixen and comply with the strict regulations of the British Civil Aviation Authority, Jones founded the De Havilland Aviation Limited in Bournemouth. His determination led to success, because since 2001 the Foxy Lady (G-CVIX) has once again been flying at numerous airshows.

In one of their hangars, the Fleet Air Arm Museum at Yeovilton has reconstructed an aircraft carrier deck, complete with bridge and catapult. One of the stars of this exhibition is the Sea Vixen FAW 2 XS590 that had been operated by 892 and 899 Squadron.

# Comeback of a veteran

## A-26B INVADER

**Type:** Medium war plane
**Crew:** 3
**Engines:** 2 Pratt & Whitney R-2800-79
**Power:** 1,470kW (2,000hp) each
**Length:** 15.47m
**Height:** 5.64m
**Wingspan:** 21.35m
**Wing area:** 50.21m²
**Empty weight:** 10,134kg
**Max take-off weight:** 16,217kg
**Max speed:** 597km/h
**Range:** 2,846km
**Service ceiling:** 6,740m
**Armament:** Four machine guns in rotating turrets, six machine guns in the nose (all 12.7mm) and a bomb load of up to 1,812kg

Mission: top secret. Several heavily armed propeller aircraft with their nationality markings painted out take off with direction Laos. Their exact orders remain unknown. Until 1969, the 609th Special Operations Squadron of the US Air Force in Thailand used a special aircraft, which had already proven its reliability during WWII as well as in Korea. As early as 10 July 1942, the first Douglas Invader took off for its inaugural flight from Mines Field, today's major Los Angeles airport. An initial test mission with this new aircraft from Britain in the summer of 1944 awoke great expectations, and as a result, from 17 November 1944 the 9th Air Force began using it for regular missions. The Invader got its infamous reputation because of its low-level attacks. Many pilots treated the bomber as a fighter plane and allegedly pulled up to 8G. After the war, the USAAF made the

*The A-26B 41-39230 (N9682C) spent its later years as a spraying plane in Kansas, when it was 'rescued' by the Confederate Air Force and renamed Vegas Vixen. This organisation of warbird enthusiasts, now called the Commemorative Air Force, also managed to acquire in 1977 another Invader with machine guns fitted in the nose (A-26B 43-7140).*

*During its active operational time, the flying characteristics of the warplane were much acknowledged by its pilots. Here, the Vegas Vixen of the Commemorative Air Force displays her true qualities.*

Invader its light standard bomber, designated it B-26 (not to be confused with its predecessor, the Martin B-26 Marauder) and used it in Korea and elsewhere. In the late 1950s, two-engine piston aircraft were increasingly replaced by jets. However, facing the guerrilla war in Vietnam, the US Air Force recommissioned the Invader. The US Air Force's very last A-26 served as a transport plane for high-ranking generals until 1972.

## WATER BOMBER

The Invader was used by many air forces. Later it served as a water bomber, racing plane and business plane. This is why there are as many as approximately 100 aircraft still in existence today, of which 30 are in an airworthy state. Eighteen of the latter are operated as water bombers by Airspray, a Canadian company based on Red Deer Airport in Alberta. The only flying Invader in Europe belongs to Scandinavian Historical Flight from Oslo. The **A-26B 44-34602 (N167B) Sugarland Express** left the Douglas hangars in 1944 and was used as a trainer by the US Air Force. Later, the aircraft was modified into a business plane; it was owned by a company from New Mexico for 20 years. In the late 1980s, the Scandinavians bought the aircraft and restored it to its original state.

The A-26C in the USAF Museum in Dayton bears the markings of 34th Bomb Squadron from the Korean War.

The two main versions of the Invader can be told apart by their noses. The A-26B was mainly equipped with up to eight machine guns in its covered nose, whereas the nose of the A-26C shown in the photograph above was fitted with a glass dome for the bomb aimer.

The final version of the Invader created some confusion. For political reasons, the Thai government didn't want any US bombers in its country so the American military quickly changed the aircraft's designation from B-26K into A-26A. Today, the 64-17653 is in the Pima Air and Space Museum.

The A-26B Invader 44-34538 (N34538) *Feeding Frenzy* flew in the early 1950s for the French Air Force (Armée de l'Air) in Indochina. In 1955, the French decommissioned the assault aircraft. Then an oil company bought the Invader and had it converted into a business plane. From 1966 to 1988, the Hughes aviation company used the aircraft for test purposes. In 1990, the 'oldie' was bought by a film producer who modified it into a camera platform. At the same time, he had it restored to its former military standard. Today the warbird is owned by Martin Aviation and based at John Wayne Airport in California.

# A dove becomes a soldier

Aeroplane engineer Igo Etrich's great success, the 'Taube' (dove), had been produced under licence by the Austrian aircraft designer Edmund Rumpler. However, their business agreements had created ill feeling. After the Imperial Patent Office had rejected the Taube's protection by patent, Rumpler no longer felt obliged to fulfil the conditions that had been imposed on his production in Berlin nor to pay the licence fees to Etrich. The whole row revolved around the special wing shape, which Etrich had copied from the winged seed of *Zanonia macrocarpa*, an exotic pumpkin species. Around the turn of the nineteenth century, the designer Etrich had begun to develop a glider according to Otto Lilienthal's example. Several setbacks could not demoralise him, and in 1909 he had created the Etrich I, his first motorised aeroplane. Unfortunately, the apparatus displayed rather poor flight characteristics and was soon replaced by the improved version Etrich II. This aeroplane took off from Vienna on 12 April 1910 for its inaugural flight and was soon to gain worldwide fame as the 'Taube'. However, at the beginning of World War I, the 500 very successful aeroplanes that had been built by Etrich, Rumpler and other manufacturers were already regarded as outdated and only saw combat action as scout planes until late 1914. The Taube was the first German World War I aeroplane to fly over Paris, where it dropped leaflets. It seems a shame that

only a handful of examples of the early years of aviation have survived to the present day. One Taube that was built by Etrich himself in 1910 can now be admired in the Technical Museum (Technisches Museum) in Vienna, and another aeroplane from the Rumpler production can be found in the German Museum (Deutsches Museum) in Munich. The Technical Museum in Oslo owns a special version of the aeroplane: a Rumpler Taube with floats. Another Taube is in store in the Polish Aviation Museum in Cracow. Apart from these originals, many other rebuilds are on display, for example in the Luftwaffe Museum in Berlin-Gatow.

*The rebuild from Fürstenwalde is powered by a 105hp Walter Minor engine.*

Towards the end of the 1990s, an airworthy rebuild of a 1913 Etrich Taube was created at the historical airfield of Fürstenwalde. In Brandenburg, the aviation enthusiast Heinz Linner from Vienna started a project for the production of historical aircraft. This was not his first project of that kind: in 1985 he had already initiated the rebuild of another Taube in Austria. With the support and funding of the Fürstenwalde Airport Operator (Flugplatz-Betriebsgesellschaft Fürstenwalde), Linner's company, the Historic Aircraft Construction (Historischer Flugzeugbau) was founded in 1998. The company's first creation, a Taube with the registration D-ETRI, made its inaugural flight on 13 May 2000 in Fürstenwalde, a historic airfield that has been in use since 1915.

## ETRICH TAUBE

**Type:** Scout plane
**Crew:** 2
**Engine:** 1 Clerget aeroengine
**Power:** 37kW (50hp)
**Length:** 10m
**Height:** 3.5m
**Wingspan:** 14m
**Wing area:** 33m²
**Empty weight:** 370kg
**Max take-off weight:** 520kg
**Max speed:** 70km/h
**Armament:** None

*The aeroplane was controlled by warping the wing and tail fins with the help of tension wires.*

# Proven warhorse

Sink the Bismarck! These were the orders given to a group of 15 ageing biplanes before they took off from the deck of HMS *Ark Royal* in the evening of 26 May 1941. But their outward appearance proved to be quite deceptive with regard to their actual efficiency: the aircraft landed two torpedo hits, which damaged the rudder system of the most famous German battleship and sealed its fate. This attack secured the Swordfish biplane its place in history. The British aircraft manufacturer Fairey, the designer of the Swordfish, had had a difficult time with his creation. The Swordfish was completely against the trend at a time when many air forces had begun to convert their fleets to full-metal monoplanes. In spite of the seemingly outdated concept, the marine aviators of the Royal Navy received their first Swordfish Mk I in July 1936. The biplane had a steel tube fuselage and fabric covering and its flight characteristics were gentle and forgiving. In total, nearly 2,400 aircraft were built. The Navy decommissioned its last Swordfish as late as 28 June 1945 – the *Stringbag* survived even its successor model, the Fairey Albacore.

## SWORDFISH MK I

**Type:** Torpedo bomber
**Crew:** 2-3
**Engine:** 1 Bristol Pegasus IIIM3
**Power:** 515kW (690hp) each
**Length:** 11.12m
**Height:** 3.76m
**Wingspan:** 13.86m
**Wing area:** 50.36m²
**Empty weight:** 1,864kg
**Max take-off weight:** 3,438kg
**Max speed:** 230km/h
**Range:** 840km
**Service ceiling:** 5,030m
**Armament:** One fixed, forward-firing machine gun, one machine gun on a Scarff ring (both 7.7mm), and a bomb load of up to 730kg

*This Swordfish Mk I was built by Blackburn, and it is the oldest existing aircraft of its type. It made its inaugural flight on 21 October 1941. Later, the W5856 was operated from Gibraltar until it went to a base in Canada and was used as a trainer. In March 1945 its military career came to an end. Afterwards the 'Blackfish' (this was the nickname for Swordfishes that were built by Blackburn) was used by two civilian operators as an agricultural plane. The oldie's next station was the Strathallan Collection in Scotland. In 1990, British Aerospace bought the biplane and restored it to an airworthy state (it had its inaugural flight on 3 May 1993). Since then it has been flying for its new owner, the Royal Navy Historic Flight.*

The development of the Swordfish had its beginnings in 1933 with the three-seater TSR I, which later crashed during spinning tests. Soon afterwards, the TSR II was created: it had a longer fuselage, increased tail surfaces and a more powerful engine. The maiden flight of the Swordfish on 17 April 1934 had just been made, when the Air Ministry ordered the first series production aircraft of the Mk I version. The photograph shows the W5856 from the first series.

The Swordfish Mk II LS326 of the RN Historic Flight can be admired regularly in flight. The aircraft was delivered on 17 August 1943 and returned to Fairey after the war. In 1960, Fairey's successor company Westland handed the biplane over to the Navy, where it has been used for flight displays up to the present day. A third aircraft will soon join the Fleet: this time it will be the Swordfish Mk III NF389, which is currently being restored by BAE Systems in Brough.

Left: The Swordfish's main weapon was a torpedo. It was one of these weapons that sealed the Bismarck's fate in 1941.

Right: The Royal Navy was so thrilled by its new acquisition that Fairey on its own was unable to satisfy further demand; so a second production line was opened at Blackburn. From 1943, Blackburn produced the Mk II, which had a reinforced lower wing to carry rockets. The photograph shows the LS326 of the RN Historic Flight.

Four airworthy Swordfishes and another 17 museum aircraft still exist today. Canada is the current home of the Swordfish Mk II HS469 (C-GRCN), which has belonged to the Shearwater Aviation Museum in Dartmouth since 1992, as well as the Mk II HS554 (C-GEVS), which is privately owned in Ontario. Some representatives of the Stringbag can be found, amongst others, in the Fleet Air Arm Museum in Yeovilton, the Imperial War Museum in Duxford as well as the Museum of Transport and Technology in Auckland, New Zealand. The aircraft shown in the photograph is displayed in the National Aviation Museum in Ottawa. To ensure easier storage of the aircraft on carriers, the wings were designed to be folded back.

# A stop-gap with a fighting spirit

The upcoming designs for monoplane fighters in the mid-1930s heralded a new era in aircraft construction. However, it was still some time before the Royal Air Force was equipped with such modern aircraft as the Hawker Hurricane or Supermarine Spitfire. So that it did not fall behind other air forces, the British Air Ministry set out to find at least a temporary solution, and a design by Gloster that had originated from a private initiative seemed to fit requirements. The prototype of the all-metal biplane made its first flight on 12 September 1934, and was able to reach a maximum speed of 400km/h – more than any other British fighter at the time. This performance secured the career of the new model, which in later years was fitted with a closed canopy. In February 1937, No. 72 Squadron received its first Gladiator Mk I, and the biplane saw its first combat action in May 1940 in France. But here it proved to be desperately inferior to the German fighter planes and suffered heavy losses. However, the RAF remained faithful to its Gladiators in the Mediterranean region and the Near East until 1941.

*There is only one remaining airworthy Gloster Gladiator left. The Mk I L8032 was delivered to the RAF in 1938. After the war had ended, the aircraft was bought privately and later restored by Gloster. In 1960, the company donated the biplane to the Shuttleworth Collection in Old Warden. Here it is flown regularly, most recently in Norwegian colours.*

## GLADIATOR MK I

**Type:** Fighter
**Crew:** 1
**Engine:** Bristol Mercury IX
**Power:** 627kW (840hp)
**Length:** 8.36m
**Height:** 3.15m
**Wingspan:** 9.83m
**Wing area:** 30.01m²
**Empty weight:** 1,565kg
**Max take-off weight:** 2,155kg
**Max speed:** 407km/h
**Range:** 547km
**Service ceiling:** 10,060m
**Armament:** Two machine guns in the nose and another two in the wings (all 7.7mm)

Gloster manufactured a total of 527 Gladiator aircraft, some of which were for export to customers in Belgium, China, Ireland, Latvia, Lithuania, Norway and Sweden. Finland used the aircraft shown in the photograph and 29 other Mk IIs in its war against the Soviet Union.

In the early 1990s the Shuttleworth fighter flew in the colours of 247 Squadron of the Royal Air Force.

Above: The Gladiator Mk II K8042 in the Royal Air Force Museum in Hendon can be distinguished from its predecessor by the three-blade propeller that replaced the former wooden two-blade version.

The Gladiator was fitted with a canopy that was high tech at the time. However, most pilots preferred to fly with an open cockpit.

# Back to the future

It could have descended from another planet: when US soldiers entered Friedrichsroda on their advance into the German heartlands, they found the world's first all-wing jet airplane in a furniture factory. The Horten IX was the futuristic prototype of the planned series version Gotha 229. The aircraft didn't really have any fuselage – the pilot was squeezed in between the two engines in the middle section of the backswept wing. In August 1943, the all-wing aircraft pioneers Walter and Reimar Horten had been personally commissioned to build the new model by Luftwaffe Commander-in-Chief Hermann Göring. The jet was to be ready for take-off in only six months' time. The inaugural flight was planned as a glider without engines because the Junkers jet engines that were destined for the new aircraft were not yet ready. But things turned out differently: the German Air Ministry (Reichsluftfahrtministerium) disbanded the Luftwaffenkommando IX, which had been set up specifically for the operation of the new all-wing jet aircraft. In spite of this serious setback, the work was continued on Göring's orders without official funding. On 1 March 1944, the H IX V-1 made its first jumps as a glider, and four days later a tow-plane took the Horten into the sky for its inaugural flight. At the same time, the Horten brothers pushed the final development of the jet-propelled H IX V-2 in Göttingen. They worked day and night, and on 2 February 1945 the second prototype took off from Oranienburg airfield. As a result the Gotha Wagon Company (Gothaer Waggonfabrik) got the order. It was to build 40 series aircraft with the designation Go 229 under licence. While the V-3 was already being built in an outsourced factory in Friedrichsroda, the short life of the V-2 came to an abrupt end: on 18 February, the right-hand jet engine stopped just before landing and the aircraft crashed. The V-1 didn't survive the war either: it was destroyed at Brandis airbase.

## GOTHA GO 229 (HORTEN IX V-3)

**Type:** Fighter-bomber
**Crew:** 1
**Engines:** 2 Junkers Jumo 004
**Power:** 9kN each
**Length:** Approx. 7.20m
**Height:** Approx. 2.60m
**Wingspan:** 16.80m
**Wing area:** 52.8m$^2$
**Empty weight:** 4,844kg
**Max take-off weight:** 6,876kg
**Max speed:** 960km/h
**Range:** 2,400km (planned)
**Armament:** Four machine cannons (planned)

*The Horten IX V-3 has been rotting for decades in a non-air-conditioned hangar of the Paul Garber Facility in Silver Hill. Even the opening of the museum's new branch on Dulles Airport is very unlikely to change the situation. The all-wing aircraft has not yet been named in the list of the aircraft that are to be restored by 2007, which is kept by the Udvar Hazy Center. Time is running out because the original wooden planking is rapidly deteriorating.*

*In Göttingen, the Horten brothers constructed the H IX V-2 nearly exclusively from wood.*

*US Army specialists transported the nearly completed V-3 from Friedrichsroda to the US for a closer inspection. They renamed the jet FE-490, but it was never completed for potential flight tests. Instead, the revolutionary aircraft was taken and put into store in the National Air & Space Museum in Silver Hill, Maryland (photograph: Adel Krämer).*

# Mighty cat

*The extravagant nose wheel is regarded as one of the Tigercat's trademarks. However, it proved to be an obstacle for the aircraft's approval for carrier operations.*

The US Navy had great plans for the Tigercat. This aircraft, with the designation F7F, finally put an end to the Navy's long search for a heavy two-engine, carrier-based fighter. But things didn't go the way they were intended: due to the combination of the aircraft's tricycle gear, its high weight, and problems with the hook design, the fighter was declared incapable of carrier operations. Instead, the US Marine Corps became interested in the aircraft, and they were to become its main operator. But a potentially great career for this promising design was delayed on many occasions, and only 364 of 650 ordered aircraft had left the production lines by the end of the war. The first combat-ready fighters arrived in Okinawa on the second last day of World War II and didn't see any action in the Far East. However, the Tigercat became somewhat better known during the Korean War, despite the fact that it was only operated by one squadron. The aircraft flew its last mission in Korea in April 1952. Nevertheless the F7F performed well in the air and was heavily armed, and in spite of its short combat career, was a valuable aircraft for the Marines, particularly in its role as a night fighter.

## A SMALL COMMUNITY

Only about twelve of Grumman's Tigercat two-engine planes still exist today, amongst them some warbirds. Most of these originate from the stocks of former fire-fighting planes. In California alone, three flying warbirds can be found: the **F7F-3 80532 (N7195C)** in Oakland, the **F7F-3P 80483 (NX6178C)** that belongs to Richard Bertea in Chino, and the **F7F-3 80412 (N207F)** of the Palm Springs Air Museum. Apart from the airworthy aircraft, the mighty Tigercat can also be admired in the following museums: National Museum of Naval Aviation of the US Navy in Pensacola, Florida; Planes of Fame Museum in Chino; Pima Air and Space Museum, Tuscon; and Weeks Air Museum in Tamiami.

## F7F-3P 80425 (G-RUMT)

The only Tigercat in Europe belongs to the Fighter Collection in Duxford. The aircraft came from the collection of David Tallichet and underwent major restoration in Chino, California, before embarking on its journey to Britain. After an epic ferry flight from the US, the aircraft landed in Duxford on 29 June 1996.

## F7F-3N 80503 (N800RW)

This night fighter entered service with the US Marine Corps on 31 July 1945. After its decommissioning, the aircraft was owned by various private individuals until it became a spare parts store for other water bombers. The 'oldie' was rescued by the Lone Star Flight Museum in Galveston, Texas, and restored to its original glory. Since then the F7F has been enriching the airshow community as Big Bossman.

*The US Marine Corps decommissioned the F7F-3P 80390 (N700F) in April 1948. The aircraft was put into storage until it was bought by George Krietzberg, who owns another 14 Tigercats. The Tigercat came cheap: George paid only 1,200 dollars for the beauty. After a few detours and several seasons as a fire-fighting plane, the fighter ended up with the Kalamazoo Aviation History Museum in Michigan in 1981.*

*Grumman's two-engine fighter was almost exclusively used by the US Marine Corps.*

## F7F-3 TIGERCAT

**Type:** Fighter
**Crew:** 1
**Engines:** 2 Pratt & Whitney R-2800-34W
**Power:** 1,544kW (2,100hp) each
**Length:** 13.83m
**Height:** 4.98m
**Wingspan:** 15.70m
**Wing area:** 42.27m²
**Empty weight:** 7,380kg
**Max take-off weight:** 11,666kg
**Max speed:** 724km/h
**Range:** 3,055km
**Service ceiling:** 12,405m
**Armament:** Four machine guns (12.7mm),
    four 20mm cannons, and various
    external loads of up to 900kg

The F7F-2 was succeeded by the third version of the Tigercat, which featured more powerful engines and an enlarged rudder. The F7F-3 was also operated as a reconnaissance plane (-3P), and as a night fighter with a bigger radar nose (-3N) like the aircraft in the photograph, which is exhibited in Chino.

The F7F-2 was the second series-production version of the Tigercat. Grumman had begun the development of a heavy fighter as early as October 1939, but it still took until 3 November 1943 before test pilot Bob Hall took off the for the inaugural flight of the first prototype.

*With regard to the magnificent flight performance of the Grumman F7F, a warbird pilot once said: 'The Tigercat climbs like a homesick angel.'*

# The avenger of Pearl Harbor

The ground crew of 8th Torpedo Squadron keeps looking to the sky, but in vain. Their six Avengers will not return to their base on Midway. The battle for this Pacific island will see its turning point in June 1942, giving the US the necessary advantage over Japan, but meanwhile the debut of the new Navy torpedo bomber has been disastrous. The Japanese have brought down five aircraft and the sixth is just able to manage a crash landing on the beach without achieving a single hit. Will this be the end of the US strategic plans? Faced with the rapid technological advance of the European nations and the Japanese, in 1939 the US Navy initiated an ambitious programme to modernise its totally outdated carrier aircraft. One of the first new designs was the TBF-1, a model by Grumman, the traditional supplier of fighters for the Navy. The new concept resembled that of an enlarged F4F Wildcat, the company's first monoplane fighter aircraft. The voluminous all-metal fuselage took a crew of three as well as the weapons bay with its hydraulic doors. At the rear end of the cockpit the designers had planned a machine-gun turret for self-defence. In August 1941, four months prior to the Japanese attack on the Navy base in Pearl Harbor, the first of the new carrier aircraft made its inaugural flight. Once it had entered service with the US forces, it was soon given the name Avenger in order to raise hopes after the defeat at Pearl Harbor. After the Midway disaster, the 'avenger' slowly began to fulfil the Navy's expectations, and developed into one of the most important US Navy aircraft of World War II. After the war, the Avenger also proved to be a very useful aircraft in non-armed operations: some were converted into surveillance planes and, as TBM-3W, were still flying as late as 1956. With its 2.4m-wide radar aerial, which was situated in an under-fuselage compartment, the aircraft were regarded as pioneers of today's airborne early warning technology.

## TBM-3E AVENGER

**Type:** Torpedo bomber
**Crew:** 3
**Engine:** 1 Wright R-2600-20
**Power:** 1,397kW (1,900hp)
**Length:** 12.48m
**Height:** 5.00m
**Wingspan:** 16.51m
**Wing area:** 45.52m²
**Empty weight:** 4,783kg
**Max take-off weight:** 8,117kg
**Max speed:** 444km/h
**Range:** 1,820km
**Service ceiling:** 9,175m
**Armament:** Two forward-firing machine guns, one machine gun in the turret (all 12.7mm), one 7.7mm machine gun in the rear lower fuselage, and a bomb load of up to 906kg in the bomb bay

*Originally, the Avenger 53319 (G-BTDP) left the production line as a TBM-3E torpedo bomber and entered service on 16 May 1945. Later on, the US Navy converted the aircraft into a TBM-3R transport plane that was used to supply aircraft carriers with mail and provisions until 1956. For this purpose, the Navy also demounted the gun turret. The retired workhorse spent the following decades mainly on the ground until it was bought by Anthony Haig-Thomas in 1987. After a major overhaul, the warbird came to Britain by ship in 1989. Today, the single-engine giant is based in North Weald.*

## WORKHORSES

Similar to the Grumman Tigercat, many of today's warbirds came from agricultural and fire-fighting companies. Until recently, seven Avengers were still being used as water bombers in New Brunswick, Canada. In early 2003, they were on sale for prices starting at 140,000 dollars. Most of the aircraft will probably find their way into warbird circles or museums, which already own quite a large number of these torpedo bombers. The majority of the airworthy planes are located in the US. In Europe, four Avengers can be found: one each in the Imperial War Museum in Duxford and the Fleet Air Arm Museum in Yeovilton, and another two that fly in private ownership, including the **Avenger 85869 (F-AZJA)**. The TBM-3E was delivered to the US Navy in March 1945 and was modified into a transport plane in 1946. After its decommissioning in 1956, the aircraft was used as a water bomber, until it was restored to its original bomber state by an enthusiast collector. Since 1989, the 'oldie' has been flying for the Association of Vintage Aeroplane Pilots & Mechanics (Association des Mécaniciens Pilotes d'Aéronefs Anciens) in Melun in France.

*Following a difficult early period while in operation, the Avenger grew into one of the most successful Navy bombers of the war and has become an essential participant in any warbird show.*

*In order to create space on the tight carrier decks, it was possible to fold the Avenger's wings back. At Oshkosh Airshow, the owner of the aircraft shown in the photograph makes use of this option.*

*An early Avenger TBF-1 of the first series-production version on a patrol flight. The 'F' indicated that the aircraft had been manufactured by Grumman. However, most of the nearly 10,000 Avengers that were built were produced by the Eastern Aircraft Division of the General Motors Corporation. This company had been specifically founded for this purpose and all Avengers built there were given the designation TBM. Because the Navy had given highest priority to the Grumman fighters, the company was forced to look for a subcontractor in order to meet the demand. The automobile giant General Motors had just suffered a production gap due to severe restrictions on civilian car production numbers and was able to offer its freed capacity to Grumman.*

*The Imperial War Museum in Duxford had its Avenger painted in the colours of the aircraft flown by former US President George Bush in World War II, father of today's President.*

# Dinosaurs in the jet age

The visitors see red. The 1960s spectacle on the apron of the tranquil airfield of Lübeck-Blankensee, with its row of fantastic aircraft on display, would have made the hearts of today's warbird enthusiasts beat faster. Side by side, the bright red Sea Furies can be admired at an open day. The German Aviation Consultancy Service (Deutscher Luftfahrtberatungsdienst) could not have chosen a more suitable aircraft as a target-tower. The Hawker Fury was, after all, one of the ultimate piston-engine fighters of World War II and was operated from Lübeck until the mid-1970s. On their constant search for increasingly more powerful aircraft designs, the engineers of Hawker, the traditional supplier of fighters for the Royal Air Force, had come up with a smaller version of the heavier Tempest by simply taking out the middle section of the wing. On 1 September 1944, the prototype of the Fury took off for its inaugural flight. However, because the war was running well for the Allies, the Royal Air Force cancelled its order in 1945. Only the marine version of the aircraft, the Sea Fury, remained. The company manufactured a total of 615 Sea Furies for the British naval aviators. They were kept in service until 1953 and served well in the Korean War. One FB Mk 11 fighter-bomber even managed to shoot down a MiG-15 jet. Several other nations also appreciated the performance of the Sea Fury, and export customers include Egypt, Australia, Burma, Iraq, Canada, Cuba, The Netherlands and Pakistan.

## SEA FURY FB MK 11

**Type:** Fighter-bomber
**Crew:** 1
**Engine:** 1 Bristol Centaurus XVIII
**Power:** 1,823kW (2,480hp)
**Length:** 10.57m
**Height:** 4.46m
**Wingspan:** 11.71m
**Wing area:** 26.00m$^2$
**Empty weight:** 4,186kg
**Max take-off weight:** 6,620kg
**Max speed:** 740km/h
**Range:** 1,126km (1,673km with additional fuel tanks)
**Service ceiling:** 10,912m
**Armament:** Four 20mm cannons and various external loads (eg two 454kg bombs)

## RACING ATMOSPHERE

Fortunately, about 60 Furies have survived their active service, which is quite a high number. Approximately 40 aircraft are in an airworthy state or are being restored to this state. Some of them came from the target-towers that were used in Germany, and others came from Iraq, brought back by warbird enthusiasts with the most enormous difficulties. Many owners in the US use the Hawker fighter as a racing plane because of its extremely powerful engine. However, European stocks of Hawker's last propeller fighter have become seriously diminished. The Royal Navy Historic Flight didn't have much luck with its aircraft: in 1989, the TF956 crashed into the sea off the Scottish coast, and the two-seater WG655 (former D-CACU) suffered a similar fate with a crash landing in July 1990. Today, the wreckage is being restored into another airworthy Fury in the US. In 1994, the memorial organisation of the British naval aviators decided to have the FB Mk 11 VR930 restored by British Aerospace (now BAE Systems) in Brough, the aircraft having previously served as a spare part donator for other Furies. Initially, huge problems caused by the Centaurus engine had to be overcome; then the Sea Fury was again ready for take-off on 1 March 2001. The Fighter Collection in Duxford is also reconstructing one of these naval fighters. The Fury of the Old Flying Machine Company (G-BTTA) came from Iraq and has now found a new home in South Africa. Paul Morgan, another Sea Fury owner (WH588/G-EEMV), died when his Fury crashed in May 2001. The last remaining Sea Fury in Germany, the single-seater FB Mk 11 D-CACY, had been displayed in the Luftwaffe Museum in Uetersen for years. However, when the museum finally moved to Berlin in 1995, a deal was struck with the Old Flying Machine Company in Duxford and the Fury was exchanged for, amongst others, a Fieseler Fi 156 Storch. The British sold the aircraft on: in 1998, Kermit Weeks from Florida bought the Sea Fury. There are two more Furies left on static display in Europe, one in the Fleet Air Arm Museum in Yeovilton and the other in the Military Aviation Museum (Militaire Luchtvaart Museum) in Soesterberg, The Netherlands.

The Fury FB Mk 10 with the serial number ISS25 came from Iraq. Ed Jurist and David Tallichet brought the exotic aircraft home from the Gulf state in the late 1970s. In the 1980s, Texan oil magnate Howard Pardue from Breckenridge acquired the Fury (NX666HP) and had the British engine replaced by a Wright R-3350 with a tuned exhaust gas system.

September Pops, a Sea Fury T Mk 20 with the registration NX233MB, is owned by Fury Limited from Carson City, Nevada.

*The Sea Fury FB Mk 11 WH587 served with the Australian naval aviators. Now, the fighter-bomber is based in California.*

Paul Morgan's Sea Fury had one of its last appearances at the ILA 2000 in Berlin. The aircraft crashed one year later.

This Sea Fury T Mk 20 spent many years in Germany. From 1960 to 1974, today's racer flew for the German Aviation Consultancy Service (Deutscher Luftfahrtberatungsdient) as a target-tower. After that, the Fury came to the US, where it was converted into a single-seater. The aircraft was extensively damaged during a hangar fire in 1988. The company Aileron, Incorporated from Illinois, has been using the WG653 (N62143) Riff Raff as a racing plane since 1997. For this purpose, the racer, which had already been fast enough by most standards, was equipped with a Wright R-3350 Cyclone, one of the most powerful piston engines in the US. The same engine was also used in the B-29.

This Fury trainer came from Burmese Air Force stocks. Since 1979, Frank Sanders has made the T Mk 20 VZ368 the focus of his racing ambitions. With the support of his family, he installed a Wright R-4360 Wasp Major: this monstrous engine was also used, amongst others, in the Convair B-36 bomber, at the time the biggest aircraft in the world. Its power in the Fury comes to more than 2,940kW (4,000hp). The engine's extraordinary power forced Sanders to increase the rudder and propeller of his Fury, and to be on the safe side, he also installed the appropriate wheel brakes from a supersonic jet. Up to now, this Fury, the Dreadnought (N20SF), has won the Reno races twice, and remains a strong candidate for the winner's rostrum. The Sanders fleet also includes the two-seater Sea Fury N924G, formerly registered as D-CAMI in Germany.

Originally, Hawker had developed the first two-seaters for Iraq. However, the aircraft shown in the photograph was delivered to Pakistan. In contrast to the T Mk 20, the two canopies were not connected with each other.

The last German Sea Fury was displayed in the Luftwaffe Museum. In 1995, it was transported to Duxford in an unusual manner: a helicopter carried it all the way to Britain as an external load.

Brian Sanders, a member of the Sanders clan, flies this fighter-bomber in air races. The Sea Fury FB Mk 11 TG114 (N232J) Argonaut had formerly been used by the Canadian naval aviators. The aircraft is owned by Marana Airplane Co. from Akron, Ohio, and is powered by a Wright R-3350. In the early 1990s, the Sea Fury spent several years in Europe (North Weald).

# Beauty in uniform

In the years following World War II, the arch rivals Douglas and Lockheed fought for lucrative airliner orders with no holds barred. While Lockheed scored with regard to technological progress, Douglas achieved considerably higher sales figures. Douglas manufactured 2,210 aircraft of its airliner series of DC-4, DC-6 and DC-7, whereas its competitor, the Lockheed Aircraft Corporation from Burbank, produced a mere 856 units of the elegant Constellation series. A large part of the orders, *ie* 55 per cent, came from the US military, which had more or less voluntarily intervened in the development of the 'Connie'. The aircraft designers from California had started with the draft for a new four-engine airliner as early as 1938. However, after the US had entered into the war, the American government prohibited the construction of civilian aircraft in order to save resources for the production of urgently needed military aircraft. But Lockheed's project seemed much too promising to be simply dropped. Therefore, the US Army Air Force ordered the aircraft as C-69. With a speed of approximately 530km/h, the transport plane was as fast as the first models of the feared Mitsubishi A6M Zero from Japan. After the war, several civilian versions were created from the C-69, until Lockheed decided to design an improved long-range model. The engineers lengthened the fuselage of the C-69 prototype by 5.62m and created the first Super Constellation with the designation 1049. The 'Super Connie' also featured a characteristic three-part tail unit and made its inaugural flight on 13 October 1950. Earlier, the US Navy had ordered six early warning aircraft of the

## RC-121D

**Type:** Early warning aircraft
**Crew:** 28 (depending on the mission type)
**Engines:** 4 Wright R-3350-34
**Power:** 2,534kW (3,447hp) each
**Length:** 35.41m
**Height:** 8.23m
**Wingspan:** 37.62m
**Wing area:** 153.66m²
**Empty weight:** 36,565kg
**Max take-off weight:** 65,136kg
**Max speed:** 516km/h
**Range:** 7,400km
**Service ceiling:** 6,280m
**Armament:** None

PO-2W type that were to bear the name *Warning Star*. In total, the Navy received 202 Super Constellations in various versions. Similar aircraft were used by the US Air Force as RC-121 and EC-121 for electronic warfare. The Air Force Reserve operated the last version, EC-121T, until its final decommissioning in October 1978. But still to the present day, its pilots remain enchanted by the *Cadillac of the Skies*, saying that the Connie was a spacious, calm, comfortable and elegant aircraft.

Possibly the most famous flying Connie of all came to the Military Air Transport Service (MATS) from Burbank in 1948. It achieved a total of 16,000 flying hours for the USAF until its decommissioning in 1968; it also took part in the Berlin Airlift. From then until 1984, the C-121A 48-0609 (N494TW) was used as a spraying plane in Canada, most recently for ConifAir Aviation with the registration C-CXKO. Then the film star and aviation enthusiast John Travolta wanted to buy and restore the 'oldie'. But in 1987 he changed his plans and sold the aircraft to Vern Raburn, a software entrepreneur from the Constellation Group. Restoration work began in August 1991, and since June 1992 the 'MATS Connie', which is now based in Avra Valley, Arizona, has been participating in airshows. Recently, the aircraft has been put up for sale for the sum of one million dollars.

The only remaining airworthy Warning Star was delivered to the USAF as RC-121D in 1955. In 1970, the aircraft was modified to EC-121T standard. The 53-0548 was said to have flown several secret missions shortly before its decommissioning in 1978. What we know for sure is that the entries for nearly 70 flying hours are missing in the logbook. The aircraft that had been in store after its active service was rescued from scrapping by the Pima Air and Space Museum in 1981. In 1994, Wayne Jones bought the Cadillac of the Skies and set up the Global Aeronautics Foundation in Camarillo for the operation of the warbird. The aircraft still had nearly all of its electronic equipment on board. Lately, flight operations of the N548GF have had to be temporarily stopped because of wing corrosion.

U. S. AIR FORCE

5
5
4

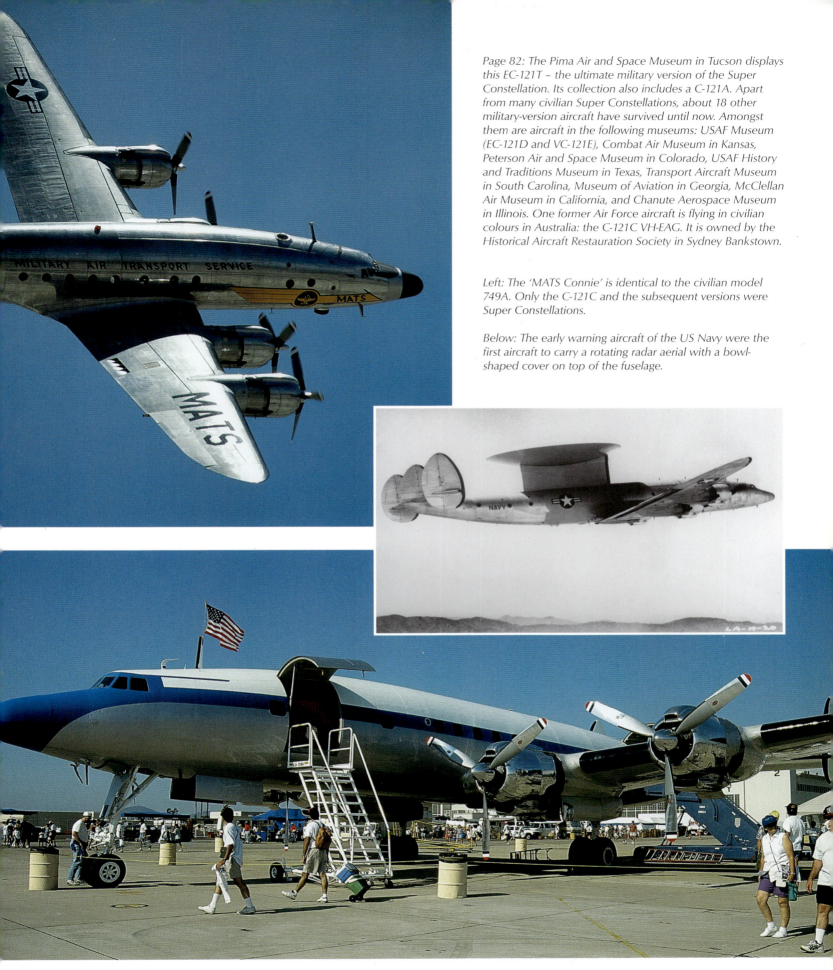

Page 82: The Pima Air and Space Museum in Tucson displays this EC-121T – the ultimate military version of the Super Constellation. Its collection also includes a C-121A. Apart from many civilian Super Constellations, about 18 other military-version aircraft have survived until now. Amongst them are aircraft in the following museums: USAF Museum (EC-121D and VC-121E), Combat Air Museum in Kansas, Peterson Air and Space Museum in Colorado, USAF History and Traditions Museum in Texas, Transport Aircraft Museum in South Carolina, Museum of Aviation in Georgia, McClellan Air Museum in California, and Chanute Aerospace Museum in Illinois. One former Air Force aircraft is flying in civilian colours in Australia: the C-121C VH-EAG. It is owned by the Historical Aircraft Restoration Society in Sydney Bankstown.

Left: The 'MATS Connie' is identical to the civilian model 749A. Only the C-121C and the subsequent versions were Super Constellations.

Below: The early warning aircraft of the US Navy were the first aircraft to carry a rotating radar aerial with a bowl-shaped cover on top of the fuselage.

The C-121C 54-0156 was received by the USAF on 1 November 1955 in Charleston, South Carolina. From then until March 1972, the aircraft flew for various units, most recently for the West Virginia Air National Guard. Until 1976, the C-121C was used as a spraying plane. After that, it was parked in the Arizona sun for six years. In December 1982, Benny Younesi bought the ageing oldie and had it ferried to California, where it was neglected once more. Finally in 1989, a group of enthusiasts of the Constellation Historical Society took care of this dilapidated beauty and restored it to its former glory. On 23 June 1994, the N73544 was once again ready for take-off.

# Fork-tail devil

Like migratory birds made from metal, large formations of unusual aircraft roar across Greenland. In August 1942, 81 fighters of 1st and 14th Fighter Group cross the Atlantic heading for Great Britain. One of these P-38F Lightnings was flown by 2nd Lieutenant Elza Shahan who remained in Iceland with his aircraft. The country was to become his new base for patrol flights. On 14 August, Shahan made history: he shot down a Focke-Wulf Fw 200 and achieved the first American air victory over a German aircraft in WWII. Later on, the 'Fork-tail devil' (Gabelschwanzteufel), as the P-38 was called by German soldiers, was mainly operated in the Pacific theatre because its two engines made the aircraft very safe, and its range was greater than that of any other US fighter at the time. The only weak spot of the Lightning was its manoeuvrability – in this regard she was clearly inferior to the much smaller Japanese fighters. The pilots therefore tried to avoid dogfights with tight turns at low speed, and as a result of these new tactics they actually downed more Japanese fighters than their comrades in other aircraft models. However, the Lightning's beginnings had been troublesome. Soon after the inaugural flight of the XP-38 on 27 January 1939, test pilot Benjamin Kelsey embarked on an attempt to set a new transcontinental record. The flight ended in a fiasco: shortly before landing at Mitchell Field in the state of New York, the aircraft lost power and Kelsey just managed a crash landing on a golf course. In spite of the accident, two and a half months later Lockheed was given the order for 13 pre-series aircraft. But problems continued, and only the P-38F, the first version that was produced in larger numbers, reached combat readiness. The Lightning was also used as a fighter-bomber, night fighter (P-38M) and reconnaissance aircraft (F-4/F-5). It was in one of these aircraft on 31 July 1944 that the famous pilot and poet Antoine de Saint Exupéry gave his life on a mission for the Free French Forces.

## EXOTIC AIRCRAFT

In spite of more than 10,000 aircraft built, the Lightning is one of the rarest US fighters to have survived to the present day; only about 15 aircraft are still in existence. Most are exhibited in museums such as the EAA Museum in Oshkosh, the Richard Bong Memorial in Wisconsin (Bong was the most successful US fighter pilot of World War II and flew the P-38), the War Eagles Air Museum in Santa Teresa, New Mexico, and Yanks Air Museum in Chino. Other Lightnings can be found on Elmendorf AFB, Alaska, in the Hill AFB Museum, Utah, and on Lackland AFB. One airworthy P-38 is in the Champlin Fighter Museum in Mesa, Arizona, but is due for ferrying to its new owner, the Museum of Flight in Seattle, in late 2003. At present, there are no Lightnings to be found in Europe: one of two remaining examples of the aircraft was in the Aviation Museum (Musée de l'Air) in Le Bourget, where it was destroyed in a fire in 1990, and the other one, P-38J California Cutie, crashed in Duxford in 1996.

### P-38F 41-7630 (N5757)
Of all the Lightnings Glacier Girl probably had the most interesting career. In 1942, the aircraft and five other P-38s as well as two B-17s were on their way to Great Britain, when the formation lost its way and all eight aircraft had to make an emergency landing on a glacier. Fifty years later to the day, a team of the Greenland Expedition Society salvaged one of the wrecks in a spectacular rescue operation. The Lightning was buried nearly 80 metres deep in the ice and had to be brought to the surface in parts through a shaft! By late 2002, the warbird, which is operated by the Lost Squadron in Middlesboro, Kentucky, had been restored and made airworthy once more.

### P-38J 44-23314 (N38BP)
Joltin' Josie is operated by the Palm Springs Air Museum in California. Since 1960 and before coming to Palm Springs, the aircraft had been exhibited in the Planes of Fame Museum in Chino. After restoration, it made its inaugural flight on 22 July 1988.

### P-38L 44-53095 (N9005R)
This Lightning came from Honduras Air Force stocks, and since 1986 it has been flying as Putt Putt Maru for the Lone Star Flight Museum in Galveston, Texas.

### P-38L 44-27083 (N2114L)
Tangerine is kept in pristine condition by the Tillamook Air Museum in Oregon.

### P-38J 44-27321 (N79123)
After the war, this Lightning was used as a racing plane. Later it was put into storage, and it was only after the aircraft's restoration had been finished in 1993 that it could take to the skies once more. Today it belongs to the Flying Heritage Collection in Bellevue, state of Washington.

### P-38L 44-26981 (N5596V)
This F-5G reconnaissance plane has had an exciting career. After its active service, the aircraft was used for civilian aerial photography; it was then handed on via 20 different owners, and restored to fighter status. It finally ended up with the Commemorative Air Force.

*White Lightnin' in action: since 1964, the P-38L 44-53254 (N25Y) has been owned by Marvin 'Lefty' Gardner from Texas. In 2001, the Lightning, which was built in 1944 and had been used as a racing plane after the war, suffered a serious blow: on a flight over Mississippi, one engine caught fire and the cockpit quickly began to fill with smoke. In spite of this hazardous situation, the pilot managed a belly landing in a cotton field. The P-38 was heavily damaged but is scheduled for restoration.*

## P-38L LIGHTNING

**Type:** Fighter
**Crew:** 1
**Engines:** 2 Allison V-1710-111
**Power:** 1,100kW (1,495hp) each
**Length:** 11.53m
**Height:** 3.91m
**Wingspan:** 15.85m
**Wing area:** 30.47m²
**Empty weight:** 5,806kg
**Max take-off weight:** 9,798kg
**Max speed:** 666km/h
**Range:** 4,185km
**Service ceiling:** 13,410m
**Armament:** One 20mm cannon, four machine guns (12.7mm) and various external loads

*In 1996, the only remaining airworthy P-38 in Europe, which is shown in the photograph in formation flight with a Lockheed F-16 Fighting Falcon at the Farnborough Airshow, crashed at Duxford.*

The P-38L 44-53097 (N3JB) has belonged to the Champlin Fighter Museum in Mesa, Arizona, since 1983.
The Lightning was built in 1944 and saw its last active service for the air forces of Cuba and Honduras.

Right: The last production version, which was also the one
with the highest production numbers, is the P-38L; it can
be distinguished from the P-38J mainly by its more
powerful engines.

The Lightning was the only US fighter to be continuously manufactured during the whole of World War II. The famous aircraft designer Clarence 'Kelly' Johnson fitted his 1937 design with two tail booms; these were to accommodate the main gear and the new exhaust gas turbochargers.

# Peacetime use of a scout plane

The Luft-Verkehrs-Gesellschaft LVG, which had been founded in Berlin-Johannesthal in 1910, produced a row of very successful single-engine scout planes like the C V. In August 1917, the company began to develop a successor model: the C VI, which was to be smaller and lighter than its predecessor. The fuselage was made of plywood and the wings were fabric-covered wooden constructions. In early February 1918, the new model finally made its inaugural flight and displayed its good flying characteristics. By the end of WWI, the LVG had built nearly 1,000 units of the aeroplane. After the war, when Germany was no longer allowed to have military aircraft, the powerful biplane was used by, amongst others, the Deutsche Luft-Reederei, a predecessor of Deutsche Lufthansa. This operator marked the former scout plane with the tail unit image of the crane – the Lufthansa symbol that has since achieved worldwide fame.

### C VI

**Type:** Scout plane
**Crew:** 2
**Engine:** 1 Benz Bz IV
**Power:** 172kW (230hp)
**Length:** 7.45m
**Height:** 2.80m
**Wingspan:** 13.00m
**Wing area:** 34.60m²
**Empty weight:** 930kg
**Max take-off weight:** 1,310kg
**Max speed:** 170km/h
**Endurance:** Approx. 3.5 hours
**Service ceiling:** 6,505m
**Armament:** Two 7.92mm machine guns (one forward-firing through the propeller disk, the other one on a Scarff ring)

*Return from a 1918 reconnaissance flight: the C VI was one of the most successful German aircraft of WWI. Apart from the aircraft that is based in Britain, there is only one other C VI, which is in the Army Museum in Brussels. The Aviation Museum (Musée de l'Air) in Le Bourget is currently restoring another aircraft, but does not have all the parts.*

*Above: The oldest remaining original aircraft from Germany that is still in flying condition has found a home at the idyllic grass strip of the Shuttleworth Collection in Old Warden.*

*Right: The LVG C VI with the works number 4503 is on loan from the Royal Air Force and has been in Old Warden since 1966. On 28 September 1972, after extensive restoration works, the rare biplane taxied to the take-off position on the Collection's meticulous lawn and took off for a new stage in its long career. Since then, the oldie (registration G-ANNJ) has participated regularly in the events of the Shuttleworth Collection.*

MESSERSCHMITT BF 109

# Record fighter

It took a top-secret letter to set in motion the development of the fighter aircraft with the highest-ever production numbers in the world. In late 1933, the German Air Ministry (Reichsluftfahrtministerium) was looking to replace its outdated biplanes as a part of the gigantic German remilitarisation programme. The civil servants had originally only included the two aircraft manufacturers Arado and Heinkel in the lucrative competition for a new fighter. Due to long-term tensions between Luftwaffe chief armament officer Erhard Milch and designer engineer Willy Messerschmitt, who had become technical director of the Bavarian Aircraft Factories (Bayerische Flugzeugwerke BFW) in 1927, the German Air Ministry initially left Messerschmitt out. German Air Minister (Reichsluftfahrtminister) Hermann Göring had to let in the lightweight construction pioneer Messerschmitt through the back door. At that moment in time, BFW would have been overstretched if it had taken on the development of a complex fighter aircraft, because the company mainly produced models of other manufacturers under licence and did not have the necessary design capacities. However, Messerschmitt used the competition aircraft Bf 108 A as a technology carrier for the Bf 109, which he developed in parallel to the other model. On 28 May 1935, the prototype of the fighter took off from Augsburg for its inaugural flight. The Bf 109 V 1 was powered by a Rolls-Royce Kestrel II because there was no suitable German engine available. Finally, in February 1936, the all-decisive test flights were performed in Travemünde. It came to a 'shoot-down' between the Bf 109 and the Heinkel He 112. Due to its superior manoeuvrability the Messerschmitt was chosen as the future Luftwaffe fighter. A little later, the first 109s that were powered by Junkers Jumo 210 D engines were used by the Legion Condor in the Spanish Civil War. Here, the aircraft saw its first combat action. II/JG 132 'Richthofen' was the first Luftwaffe unit to be equipped with the new model. From 1937 onwards, Messerschmitt fitted its aircraft with the Daimler-Benz DB 601 engine. On 11 November 1937, a tuned prototype with increased engine power set a new world speed record of 610.95km/h.

## BF 109 G-6

**Type:** Fighter
**Crew:** 1
**Engine:** 1 Daimler-Benz DB 605
**Power:** 1,342kW (1,800hp)
**Length:** 9.02m
**Height:** 3.40m
**Wingspan:** 9.92m
**Wing area:** 16.05m²
**Empty weight:** 2,656kg
**Max take-off weight:** 3,150kg
**Max speed:** 621km/h
**Range:** 720km
**Service ceiling:** 11,750m
**Armament:** Two 13mm machine guns and three 20mm cannons

The first production-series version Bf 109 E was also equipped with this engine and was mainly used in the Battle of Britain. In total, more than 4,000 units of the Bf 109 E (for 'Emil') left the production lines. Messerschmitt's designer teams improved the aerodynamic characteristics of the next version Bf 109 F, which was delivered to the fighter squadrons from spring 1941. About a year later, the Bf 109 G replaced the F version. The G for 'Gustav' was produced in a total of 82 different models, which turned spare parts supply into a nightmare for both the industry and the Luftwaffe. But these problems didn't stop the use of this successful fighter, which was manufactured right to the end of the war. The aircraft was held in such high esteem that even after 1945 further models were built in other countries. In Czechoslovakia, the company Avia manufactured the fighter with the designation S.199, while Messerschmitt's great success made its stay even longer in Spain. Here, Hispano assembled the fighter, which was called HA-1112 and fitted with Rolls-Royce Merlin engines. Only in 1967 were these Spanish aircraft taken out of service.

*Probably the best known 'Me 109' now belongs to the Messerschmitt Foundation (Messerschmitt-Stiftung) and is operated by the aerospace group EADS in Manching. In the late 1970s, EDAS' predecessor Messerschmitt Bölkow Blohm (MBB) intended to use a Bf 109 as its memorial aircraft. The company got hold of a Spanish-built HA-1112 airframe and equipped it with a DB 605 engine. After a major overhaul and a huge amount of restoration work, on 23 April 1982 the Bf 109 G-6 (D-FMBB) was once again ready for take-off.*

## HIGHLY SOUGHT-AFTER OBJECTS

Museums as well as collectors and warbird operators queue up to buy a real Messerschmitt Bf 109. Over the past few years in particular, the number of available aircraft has been increased by the salvage and restoration of several wrecks. Further restoration projects are currently being carried out. The oldest remaining 'Emil' is displayed in the German Museum (Deutsches Museum) in Munich, and soon an E-3 will be exhibited in the German Technology Museum (Deutsches Technik-Museum) in Berlin. Another E-3 can be found in the Swiss Aviators Museum (Schweizer Fliegermuseum) in Dübendorf. The Imperial War Museum in Duxford has owned a Bf 109 E-3 since the late 1990s. Another E-3 is in the National War Museum in Johannesburg, South Africa, which also owns a Bf 109 F-4, and the RAF Museum in Hendon displays one E-3 as well. An F-4 can be found in the National Aviation Museum in Ottawa, and a G-2 in the Aviation Museum in Belgrade. The Aviation Museum (Luftfahrtmuseum) in Hannover-Laatzen acquired a wrecked Bf 109 G-2 and restored it completely. In Italy, a G-4 was restored, which came to Germany on loan and was displayed in the Technology Museum (Technik-Museum) in Speyer. If the necessary funding for the purchase of the old fighter can be raised, the aircraft may well stay in Germany. The National Air and Space Museum in Washington D.C., the Australian War Memorial in Canberra as well as Utti Airbase and the Aviation Museum in Tikkakoksi (both in Finland) all have a G-6 version on display. One G-10 each is exhibited in the USAF Museum in Dayton, the Evergreen Aviation Museum, Oregon, and the Planes of Fame Museum (at its Grand Canyon branch). However, many institutions resorted to Spanish aircraft, which were then refitted with DB engines. Aircraft that have been modified in this manner are to be found at the EADS plant in Augsburg, on Wittmund Airbase (home of JG 71 Richthofen), in the Automobile and Technology Museum (Auto und Technik Museum) in Sinsheim and the Luftwaffe Museum in Berlin-Gatow.

### Bf 109 E-7 Weiße 14 (NX81562)

Currently, only one airworthy Bf 109 exists in its original state. It is said that the legendary German fighter pilot Hans-Joachim Marseille had flown this 'Emil' over France. Later on, the aircraft fought along the Eastern Front, where German troops left it behind after a crash landing in Russia. In the early 1990s, the Bf 109 and several other wrecks returned from Russia to the West. When the aircraft was on offer, David Price, head of the Museum of Flying in Santa Monica, didn't think twice: he had the Bf 109, which was built by Arado in Warnemünde, restored in Britain. The second inaugural flight was made on 9 October 1999 in California.

### Bf 109 G-10/ HA-1112 (D-FDME)

In the early 1980s, the transport entrepreneur Hans Dittes from Mannheim got a Hispano, which had flown in Germany for a while, back home from Spain. Later on, Dittes decided to update the aircraft to Bf 109 G-10 standard. His efforts proved to be successful: on 23 March 1995, the 'Dittes-Me' took off from Mannheim. For insurance reasons, the Bf 109 was temporarily operated by the Old Flying Machine Company in Duxford until it got damaged in an accident while taxiing in 1998. Someone who was coming to the rescue made the situation worse by driving his VW bus over the aircraft's wing! After the fighter had been repaired, it was bought by EADS to be displayed side by side with the Messerschmitt Foundation's G-6.

In December 1994, the Cavanaugh Flight Museum bought from Charles Church the Hispano HA-1112 C4K-172, which had been known by its last registration G-HUNN. Currently, it is based in Texas with the registration N109GU.

The US Air Force Museum in Dayton can be proud of its masterfully restored Bf 109 G-10, which carries the markings of Jagdgeschwader 300. In 1945, the aircraft had been captured by US troops on Neubiberg airfield.

A 'Bf 109' that is really a Hispano HA-1112 can be admired in the Planes of Fame Museum in Chino. The aircraft (registration NX700E) participated in the epic film Pearl Harbor. Unfortunately, after returning from a filming session, it veered off the runway during touchdown and suffered serious damage. The photograph shows the intact aircraft before the accident.

*A total of more than 33,000 Messerschmitts (the photograph shows a Bf 109 F-4) were built not only in Germany but also in Spain and Czechoslovakia: this makes the Messerschmitt the No. 1 of all fighter aircraft ever built.*

*Walter Eichhorn pilots* Fox Mike Bravo Bravo *over Manching Airbase. On 3 June 1983, the original memorial aircraft was destroyed during take-off from Neuburg Airbase. The 'oldie' had been extremely well liked, which prompted the aerospace company MBB to look for a suitable successor. Finally, on 23 June 1986, after a Hispano airframe had been found and the aircraft had been completely restored, the second inaugural flight of the 'Gustav' was made. In the long term, the Bf 109 G-6 will be replaced in its role as a demonstration aircraft by Hans Dittes' G-10.*

*The Bf 109 E-4 in the Champlin Fighter Museum is really a Spanish aircraft that was fitted with an intact DB 601 engine and an original engine cowling by the company Williams from Günzburg in the 1970s.*

The world-famous Black Six, a Bf 109 'Gustav', had been the only flying original 109 for many years. The aircraft was built by Erla in Leipzig in 1942. During its African tour of duty, the aircraft was captured by Allied troops and transported to Britain. It took experts nearly 20 years to restore the fighter before the Bf 109 G-2 Schwarze 6 (Black Six), registration G-USTV, took off for its second inaugural flight on 17 March 1991. The aircraft has been, and still is, owned by the Royal Air Force, which allowed other British operators to fly it until 1994. This permit was prolonged for another three years. Finally, on 12 October 1997, the aircraft made its last flight before retiring into a museum. And at this point disaster struck: during landing, the fighter made an unintended turn on itself due to the engine torque effect and was seriously damaged. But in spite of this, the British decided to carry out a second restoration, although this time it was to be a static one: since March 2002, the Black Six has been exhibited in the RAF Museum in Hendon.

*In Manching, the EADS maintenance experts take loving care of their '109'.*

*This Buchon, as the Spanish called their Hispano HA-1112, had been flying for the Old Flying Machine Company as G-BOML. In September 1999, Mark Hanna, a member of the OFMC, died in a crash with the fighter in Spain.*

# Doolittle's masterpiece

This was the beginning of a suicide mission into the enemy's heartland: take-off with heavy two-engine bombers from the alarmingly short flight deck of an aircraft carrier. On 18 April 1942, without a chance of returning to his ship, Lieutenant Colonel James Doolittle takes off from USS *Hornet* with his B-25B. Behind him, another 15 Mitchell bombers climb into the sky. With a take-off weight of 14 tons, the aircraft are heavier than any other carrier aircraft ever operated before them. They just make it off the deck. Without escort, they fly towards Japan, and eventually drop their bombs in low-level flight over Tokio and Nagoya. Despite the negligible military impact of the mission, the American public celebrates the attack. Up to this point in time, the US had suffered serious defeats at the hands of the Japanese forces. The symbolic attack on Japan fulfilled its purpose and gave the Americans new hope.

The 'Doolittle Raiders' in their Mitchell bombers would also have needed an awful lot of hope. Their plan to make it to airfields in China after the attack, which had been risky from the start, went wrong: due to fuel shortage, none of the aircraft reached their destination, and the crews either made crash landings or jumped from their aircraft over Japanese-held territory. But in spite of the adverse circumstances, most airmen were rescued.

Still today, the 'Doolittle Raiders' and their machines are regarded as heroes in the US. This made up for the early days of the B-25's career, which didn't start off that well. In 1938, the North American Aviation Inc. (NAA) had responded to a demand by the US Army Air Corps for a two-engine bomber, and this had produced the new NA-40. This aircraft had an unusual tandem-like arrangement for the pilots and already had some features that would subsequently be found in the B-25: the NA-40's end-plate tail unit, engine nacelles and nose gear were used for the Mitchell. The rest of the aircraft was simply a disaster: the NA-40 was too slow and had extreme vibration problems, and it finally crashed during a test flight. However, the company management wasn't going to be discouraged and its engineers came up with the larger version NA-62 which, due to its slim fuselage, was much faster than its unfortunate predecessor. Their perseverance paid off. On 10 September 1939, the military signed a contract for the delivery of 24 aircraft with the designation B-25.

Due to the extensive pre-series construction work, no prototype was built. On 19 August 1940, the B-25 took off for its inaugural flight. The designers amended the stability problems that had occurred during test flights by fitting larger end plates to the tail unit and giving the wing its characteristic slight bend. From mid-1941, the first units of the bomber were delivered to 17th Bombardment Group.

In honour of the WWI veteran William Mitchell, an unshakeable supporter of military aviation, the Air Corps

## B-25J MITCHELL

**Type:** Medium bomber
**Crew:** 6
**Engines:** 2 Wright R-2600-29 Cyclone
**Power:** 1,250kW (1,700hp) each
**Length:** 16.31m
**Height:** 4.97m
**Wingspan:** 20.61m
**Wing area:** 56.6m$^2$
**Empty weight:** 8,847kg
**Max take-off weight:** 15,855kg
**Max speed:** 471km/h
**Range:** 1,267km
**Service ceiling:** 7,380m
**Armament:** Twelve 12.7mm machine guns and a bomb load of up to 1,812kg

*A slice of history for 325,000 dollars? Wiley Sanders'
B-25J 44-86797 (N3438G) has recently been for sale.*

(named US Army Air Corps as of 20 June 1941) gave its new aircraft the name 'Mitchell'. General Mitchell didn't live to receive this belated honour. He had died in 1936 and was remembered for his consistent promotion of an independent and powerful Air Force. Mitchell had even been suspended from duty for five years because of his criticism of training standards for American aviators.

## AIR POWER

There is no other old bomber that has more remaining aircraft than the Mitchell. We know of approximately 140 aircraft, 60 of which are displayed in museums and more than 40 still in flying condition. Most of those can be found in the US and are of B-25J standard. Three Mitchells are still flying in Europe. One of them is the **B-25J 44-29507 (N320SQ)**, built in 1944 and which was used as a transport plane by the US Air Force until 1958. After having had several other owners, including a fishery company, the B-25J ended up with the Duke of Brabant Air Force. This is a group of aviation enthusiasts who are keen to promote historical aviation to the public. Their B-25J Mitchell is based in Eindhoven and is currently operated in the colours of No. 18 Squadron (Royal Australian Air Force). This aircraft was once flown by Dutch pilots in the Far East as a B-25C 'Sarinah'. Two other Mitchells can be found in The Netherlands: one B-25D in the War and Resistance Museum in Overloon and one B-25J in the Military Aviation Museum (Militaire Luchtvaart Museum) in Soesterberg. Apart from these warbirds, there is the airworthy B-25J F-AZID, kept in store in Dijon for quite some time but which was recently put up for sale for the sum of 375,000 dollars. One B-25J each is to be found in Monino in Russia and in the Aviation Museum (Museo del Aire) in Madrid in Spain. Britain is proud to exhibit one B-25J each in the Imperial War Museum in Duxford and the RAF Museum in Hendon.

The only B-25H worldwide that is still flying justifiably carries the name Gunship. In 1981, this rare version was taken from a farm in Illinois by the Weary Warriors Squadron and brought to Rockford, where restoration works began. In the 1950s and 1960s, the aircraft had been operated by the aviation company Bendix as Barbie III 43-4106 (N5548N). During the restoration work, which was completed in 1991, the friends of the Mitchell equipped the bomber with the infamous 75mm cannon in the nose section. During its active service, the 2.6m long artillery piece was regarded as very ineffective because after each shot it needed reloading by hand by a member of the crew.

*Gallant fighter: originally, the B-25D 43-3634 (N3774) of the Yankee Air Museum had been flying for the Royal Canadian Air Force. Currently the museum is equipping Gallant Warrior with a glass nose.*

*The oldest surviving Mitchell was the fourth aircraft to leave the production lines, and joined the 17th Bomb Group of the US Army Air Corps in February 1941. From 1943, the B-25 40-2168, which was still equipped with the straight wing, served as the personal transport plane for General Henry 'Hap' Arnold, Commander-in-Chief of the US Army Air Forces. After the war, the exotic bomber had several owners, amongst them the aviation pioneer and entrepreneur Howard Hughes. The Mitchell underwent restoration work on several occasions. This was carried out by the specialists of Aero Trader from California, and since then the aircraft has been flying for various operators as Proud Mary and The General. Now, its colourful history seems to have come to a temporary halt. The aircraft has been bought by the American Airpower Museum in Farmingdale, state of New York, whose president Jeff Clyman actually owns the bomber, which has been named Miss Hap after General Arnold.*

*The Fighter Collection's B-25D KL161 (G-BYDR) is one of two remaining aircraft of this version in flying condition worldwide; it is stationed on the warbird airfield in Duxford. On 19 January 1945, North American handed the bomber over to the Royal Canadian Air Force, who used it as a trainer and target-tower until 1962. After that, the bomber was to be operated as a water bomber. However, these plans didn't materialise and the aircraft's odyssey finally ended in Fairbanks, Alaska. There the Mitchell was spotted, rotting away, by the company Aero Trader from Chino, and rescued. On 8 November 1987, after a nine-hour flight via Newfoundland, Grumpy, named after a dwarf from Disney's version of Snow White, arrived at its new home.*

Austria's pride is the B-25J 44-86893 (N6123C). The aircraft was built in 1945 in North American's Kansas plant and never saw any action during WWII. After its active service, it served as a water bomber in Arizona. Later on, the bomber was parked in Mesa for a while. It was only in 1978 that a group of aircraft enthusiasts of Kansas City Warbirds Inc. showed mercy towards the old fighter, and subsequently flew it as Fairfax Ghost. In 1997, after a complete overhaul, the bomber joined the Flying Bulls, a subsidiary of the drinks manufacturer Red Bull. Today, the B-25J from Salzburg is a much admired guest at many airshows.

The B-25J 44-30801 (N30801) belongs to Ed Schnepf from Fresno, California. The J version proved to be the most successful of all Mitchell models, as well as the one with the highest production numbers (4,390 aircraft). The aircraft was not only used as a bomber with a glass nose but also as a low-level, close air support plane with nose covering and a total of 18 machine guns.

# Breakthrough into the jet era

It may well be that German engineers were responsible for launching the first US sweptback fighter. When jet fever broke out all over the world towards the end of WWII, the Californian aircraft designers of North American had already prepared a suitable study for the military. The NA-134 was based on proven technology and featured straight wings and a short and round fuselage with a nose air inlet. However, the XP-86 in its original shape would never have been able to achieve the required maximum speed of 965km/h. The solution to the problem came with the idea of the sweptback wing. Up to this point, this concept had been paid little attention and therefore seen little research in the US. Only when German research results, which had been found after the end of WWII, were investigated more closely, was the necessary data provided. After heated discussions, the military approved of the new configuration, and as soon as 20 December 1946, 33 series aircraft were ordered. On 1 October 1947, test pilot George Welsh made the inaugural flight with the futuristic jet. The aircraft was not going to disappoint its customers. On 15 September 1948, Major Richard Johnson set a new world speed record of 1,089km/h. About half a year later, in February 1949, the 1st Fighter Group at March AFB was equipped with the new fighter with the sweptback wing. The unit's officers had a naming competition and chose 'Sabre' as the official designation of the F-86. In the meantime, the engineers had been working on an improved version of the aircraft: the F-86E. This aircraft was sent directly into combat in the Korean War. In Korea, jets from East and West fought dogfights for the first time. On 17 December 1950, Lieutenant Colonel Bruce Hinton claimed the first 'kill' of a MiG-15. Later on, another, more modern version replaced the older Sabre models. The F-86F had an improved manoeuvrability, which balanced the advantage that was previously held by the MiG-15. As late as spring 1970, the last aircraft of the ultimate version F-86H were decommissioned by the Air National Guard. The Sabre was part of the equipment of nearly 40 air forces throughout the world. Including the aircraft that were manufactured under licence in Italy, Japan, Canada and Australia, a total of more than 9,000 Sabres were built, some of which flew for the new Luftwaffe.

## F-86F SABRE

**Type:** Fighter
**Crew:** 1
**Engine:** 1 General Electric J47-27
**Power:** 27.09kN
**Length:** 11.44m
**Height:** 4.47m
**Wingspan:** 11.67m
**Wing area:** 26.76m²
**Empty weight:** 4,940kg
**Max take-off weight:** 9,230kg
**Max speed:** 1,118km/h
**Range:** 2,044km (with additional fuel tanks)
**Service ceiling:** 14,630m
**Armament:** Six machine guns (12.7mm) and two external load stations for one 454kg bomb each

The audience holds its breath during a flying display of Dale Snodgrass' Sabre. The former Navy pilot has more than 4,800 flying hours on the Grumman F-14 Tomcat. The operation of the F-86F 52-4959 (N86FR) is sponsored by the telecommunications company AT&T, while the aircraft is privately registered in Florida.

The only remaining F-86A still flying is the oldest airworthy Sabre of all models ever built, and is ironically at home in Europe. On 18 April 1949, the 48-0178 entered service with the 1st Fighter Group at March AFB in California. Later on, the jet joined the Air National Guard, where it was operated until 1958. After decommissioning, the aircraft was exhibited at a school for decoration purposes; finally it was bought by a collector. In the early 1970s, warbird enthusiast Ben Hall came across the jet and decided to restore it to its original glory. On 24 May 1974, the aircraft took off for its second inaugural flight over the state of Washington. In 1990, the British foundation Golden Apple Trust became interested in the Sabre. It wanted to use the aircraft to remind people of outstanding technical achievements. The 'oldie' was operated by the Old Flying Machine Company in Duxford until 1998. After an extensive overhaul, the G-SABR has been operational once more since June 2002.

This Sabre Mk 6 was Canadian-built. From 1989 to 1994 the aircraft, together with several other jets of the same type, was operated as a target-tower on Sardinia on behalf of the military by Corporate Jets from Scottsdale, Arizona. After this mission, some of the aircraft returned to the US. Today, the N50CJ is registered privately in Tennessee, while the N30CJ was acquired by warbird pilot Jimmy Rossi. He flew the aircraft as '23711' at airshows until, in November 2002, he died when it crashed.

This 1952-built jet fighter was bought by Terence Klingele from Belleville, Illinois, from Texas Air Command in Arlington, so that it could become part of his company AirShow MiGs. Together with a MiG-15, dogfights were simulated. Recently the F-86F 52-4666 (N860AG) was for sale.

# Wild Horse

A US Senate inquiry committee once described the Mustang as the 'fighter with the most perfect aerodynamics' in the world. The design team of North American Aviation Inc. (NAA) had indeed built an airframe with such a low drag that the P-51 made history as one of the fastest fighters of WWII. However, the most famous

In Australia, the Commonwealth Aircraft Corporation built the Mustang under licence with the designation CA-18. In 1969, one of these machines found its way to the Philippines. After a crash in Manila, it was bought by OFMC founder Ray Hanna from Britain who had the fighter restored in Hong Kong. After its second inaugural flight in February 1985, the A68-192 (G-HAEC) Big Beautiful Doll was airlifted to Britain. From then, the Mustang flew for the OFMC in Duxford until it was acquired by Rob Davies.

fighter plane of the US Army Air Force (USAAF) may never have been built at all had it not been for the intervention of the British. Weakened by the Battle of Britain, the Royal Air Force was searching for a successor for the Curtiss P-40, which could strengthen the dwindling forces of the Fighter Command. The British approached NAA boss James Howard Kindelberger, who presented them with a concept that had already been created for other possible customers. The British procurement committee liked the fighter concept but demanded that the aircraft be built as fast as possible. North American managed to assemble the prototype of the NA-73X in a record-breaking 117 days. In order to enable the inaugural flight on 26 October 1940, the engineers were forced to borrow a pair of wheels from the T-6 trainer. As early as April 1941, the first Mustang I fighters for the RAF, equipped with the Allison V-1710 engine, left the production line. The USAAF also tested the new fighter. Although the test pilots were thrilled with the new aircraft, no significant order volumes were placed, and it was only after the attack on Pearl Harbor that a first batch of 150 aircraft was ordered. In spite of its good characteristics, the first refinements were soon made to the 'Wild Horse'. In particular the fighter's performance in high altitude in the battle against German fighter planes needed to be improved. As there was no time for a further development of the V-1710 engine, the NAA resorted to Rolls-Royce's Merlin, which was to be produced by the Packard Motor Car Company in the US. After this, the Army Air Force became ecstatic about the resulting P-51B, and Army Air Force Commander-in-Chief Henry Arnold immediately demanded 2,000 aircraft. On 6 March 1944, for the first time several P-51Bs escorted a bomber formation on its flight to Berlin. The next model P-51D had a so-called 'bubbletop' canopy, which gave the pilots their much desired 360-degree view, and this model finally achieved the breakthrough for the Mustang. Nearly 8,000 aircraft of this version were manufactured by NAA. In the heyday of wartime manufacturing, the men and women working for the Californian manufacturer assembled nearly 28 aircraft every day. However, the last version of the P-51 came too late to play any significant role in World War II: with its 779km/h, the P-51H could have easily become the fastest of all series Mustangs. However, this didn't mean the end for the successful Anglo-American co-production, and it wasn't until March 1957 that the aircraft, which was then designated F-51, was finally taken out of service by the US Air National Guard. Before then, the Mustang had still been very effective during the Korean War. Some units even returned their brand-new jets in exchange for their old Mustangs because they were more effective in the fighter-bomber role. As late as 1967, the US Air Force commissioned the company Cavalier Aircraft with modernising twelve of these machines for the operation in South American countries.

## P-51D MUSTANG

**Type:** Fighter
**Crew:** 1
**Engine:** 1 Packard/Rolls-Royce V-1650-7 Merlin
**Power:** 1,095kW (1,490hp)
**Length:** 9.83m
**Height:** 4.16m
**Wingspan:** 11.29m
**Wing area:** 21.64m²
**Empty weight:** 3,227kg
**Max take-off weight:** 5,481kg
**Max speed:** 699km/h
**Range:** 3,328km (with two additional fuel tanks)
**Service ceiling:** 12,800m
**Armament:** Six 12.7mm machine guns

## MUSTANG AIR FORCE

Today, North American's 'Wild Horse' is among the most popular and most numerous warbirds worldwide. There are still more than 150 aircraft flying (13 of them in Europe), which is more than the number on display in museums.

### P-51D Mustang 44-73419 (G-BTCD) Ferocious Frankie

This Mustang was built in Inglewood and entered service with the US Army Air Force on 27 February 1945. Then the aircraft was shipped to Great Britain. After about a year with the 8th Air Force, the fighter returned to the US. It was briefly put into store and then handed over to the Royal Canadian Air Force. After its military career was over, the Mustang was used as a civilian racing plane. In 1980, it changed owners once more when the Fighter Collection acquired the fighter and brought it back to Britain. In 1981, the aircraft was first shown in flight by Ray Hanna, founder of the Old Flying Machine Company (OFMC). Ray's son Mark bought the P-51D in 1999, and today the Mustang travels all over Europe as part of the Breitling Fighters.

### P-51D Mustang 44-73339 (G-SIRR)

This Mustang was owned by the musician David Gilmour of Pink Floyd. Before, the aircraft had been operated by the Texas Air National Guard and the Indonesian Air Force. After a crash, the wreck was rebuilt by experts from Chino who used parts of a former Canadian P-51 for the restoration work. On 14 February 1991, the fighter arrived at its new home in North Weald.

### P-51D Mustang 44-72216 (G-BIXL) Miss Helen

Robert Lamplough's 'oldie' is also based in a hangar in North Weald. Like another Mustang that has recently come to Duxford, Miss Helen flew for the USAAF during World War II. After that, the aircraft served with the Swedish and Israeli Air Forces.

### P-51D Mustang 44-72773 (G-SUSY) Susy

Until the 1950s, this Mustang, which belongs to Paul Morgan from Sywell, served as an F-51D with the US Air Force, most recently with the 131st Fighter Squadron and the Texas Air National Guard.

### P-51D Mustang 44-63864 (G-CBNM)

This Mustang joined the Fighter Collection in Duxford in 2002. The aircraft came from Sweden where it had been operated by Leif Jaraker as SE-BKG. During its active service with the USAAF in WWII, the Mustang shot down two Messerschmitt Me 262s. After the war it was given to the Swedish Air Force, and in the 1950s it fought for Israel.

### Mustangs in France

The crash of P-51D F-AZFI in 1998 further reduced the French Mustang community. P-51D 44-72035 (F-AZMU) Jumpin' Jacques, which had been owned by Jacques Bournet, was originally from Columbia. During the 2002 season, the aircraft, which was operated by Aero-Retro in St. Rambert, stayed grounded due to increased insurance premiums; then in early 2003 it was sold to Britain. Recently, René Bouverat's P-51D 44-74506 (F-AZJJ) Juliette was up for sale. However, after an overhaul in the US the aircraft has returned to France. Finally P-51D 44-74427 (F-AZSB) Nooky Booky IV of JCB Aviation has been flying in Nimes since 1999. This aircraft once belonged to the North American Rockwell Corporation and the legendary airshow pilot Bob Hoover.

### P-51D Mustang 44-73877 (N167F) Old Crow

After several years as a trainer in the US, the 'Norwegian' served in the Royal Canadian Air Force from 1951 to 1958. After that, it was passed on between several private owners in Canada and the US. In 1980, the Norwegian Anders Saether from Oslo bought the warbird and over a period of five years had it overhauled in Colorado. Since its ferry flight on 27 June 1986, the aircraft has been flying for the Scandinavian Historic Flight.

### P-51D Mustang 44-63507 (N51EA) Double Trouble Two

This Mustang is flown in Switzerland for Max Vogelsang's Basel-based Swiss Warbirds. The aircraft came from Canadian stocks. In 1968 it suffered a serious crash, but was rebuilt from parts of another Mustang and restored into an airworthy fighter. It then came to Europe after an intermediary stay of several years in the US.

### P-51D Mustang 44-74425 (N11T) Damn Yankee

After its eight-year service with the Royal Canadian Air Force, the Yankee went through a real odyssey. It had a total of 23 owners and survived two crashes. Since 1994, the collector's piece has been flying for Tom van de Meullen from Lelystad airfield in The Netherlands.

### P-51K Mustang 44-12852 (N357FG) Frenesi

Today, one of three remaining K-series Mustangs in flying condition belongs to James Beasley from Philadelphia. Directly after the war, the Mustang began a career as a racing plane, but in 1946 had a crash landing in Cleveland during a race. Later on, the aircraft took shadowy paths to join the Air Force of the Dominican Republic until it returned to warbird circles in the US. Another P-51K is owned by the actor Tom Cruise (N51EW Montana Miss).

Mad Max is one of approximately 150 flying Mustangs in the world. From 1969, the P-51D 45-11559 had been operated by the El Salvador Air Force. Today it has found a somewhat quieter home as Max Chapman's warbird N51MX in Florida.

Above: This P-51D 45-11525 was rescued from Indonesia by warbird enthusiasts. After its return to the US, the aircraft was flying for the War Eagles Air Museum in Santa Teresa, New Mexico. Currently the Val Halla (N151AF) is owned by Bill Anders, a former astronaut aboard Apollo 8. Here, the Mustang takes off together with Chuck Hall's Six Shooter (N2580). The 67-22580 once flew as a Cavalier Mk 2 for the Bolivian Air Force.

Left: A total of 135 Mustangs are registered in the US alone. This means that the P-51 is one of the most popular warbirds ever made.

During WWII, the legendary pilot Chuck Yeager flew a Mustang called Glamorous Glen III. Naturally, a Mustang in the correct colour scheme has to be part of the warbird community. Unfortunately, in September 2001 the P-51D 45-11381 (N551CB) crashed due to an engine failure.

Left: A Mustang pilot proudly presents his original uniform.

The P-51D Mustang 45-11518 (G-MSTG) Janie was built in 1945. It came from New Zealand and is now based in Harwick. The aircraft was stored for several decades until the Alpine Fighter Collection from Wanaka began with its restoration. This was finally completed by the aircraft's new owner Maurice Hammond in Britain.

The oldest airworthy Mustang in the world entered service with the USAAF on 1 May 1943 and was used for cold weather tests in Alaska. After approximately 56 flying hours, the P-51A 43-6006, which was equipped with the Allison engine, crashed on 16 February 1944. The wreck was salvaged in 1977 by Waldon Spillers from Ohio who restored it in great detail over a period of eight years. In July 1985 the aircraft, with the appropriate name Polar Bear, was able to take off once again. Ten years after that, in 1995, Gerald Gabe from Hollister, California, the current owner of the fighter, bought the Mustang (N51Z).

Terry Bland's red racing plane has been the most successful racer of the past few years, and has been able to take home the national championships in Reno for the fifth time so far. When the P-51D 44-74966 (N5410V) Dago Red appeared for the first time in the racing Mecca of Reno in Nevada in 1982, it claimed an immediate victory. Its pilots Skip Holm and Bruce Lockwood then took it from one victory to another: in 1998, 1999, 2000 and 2002 no other aircraft was able to keep up with it. (In 2001, the National Championship Air Races were cancelled due to the terror attacks in the US.) In order to make the Mustang as lightweight and as aerodynamic as possible, the racing experts cut off the wing tips and fitted it with a smaller canopy. With 832km/h, the racer holds the speed record over the 15 kilometres distance.

The beginnings of a legend: this photograph shows the NA-73X, the very first P-51. With a total of 16,000 aircraft built, the Mustang remains one of the most successful fighter aircraft of all times. The bomber crews of the US Army Air Force called it affectionately their 'little friend' because, due to its enormous range, the Mustang was able to escort them in their bombers over great distances.

# A fiery legend

The designer Reginald J. Mitchell's masterpiece, the Spitfire, was one of the biggest successes for the British aerospace industry. Previously, Mitchell had only ever developed one other fighter for Supermarine. This earlier aircraft, the low-wing monoplane Type 224, had a rigid gear and an open cockpit. But because of its weak performance it couldn't compete with the Gloster Gladiator and remained a one-off prototype. Mitchell's second attempt incorporated his own huge experience from building Schneider Trophy racing planes, and resulted in an aircraft with a narrow wing profile and elliptical wing tips. Rolls-Royce also played a major role in the subsequent success of the fighter. As early as 1933, the engine designers had begun to develop the Merlin engine, which was to become one of the best ever aircraft engines. At the time of the Spitfire's inaugural flight on 5 March 1936, nobody had yet thought of the numerous opportunities for development that the Spitfire's robust design would offer in the years to come – possibly with the exception of Mitchell himself. The British Air Ministry's order of 310 aircraft was like warm summer rain for the small Southampton-based company. On the other hand, this unexpected blessing brought its own problems: Supermarine was totally overstretched with the sheer number of aircraft to be manufactured, and had to licence its production to

| SPITFIRE MK VB | |
| --- | --- |
| **Type:** Fighter | |
| **Crew:** 1 | |
| **Engine:** 1 Rolls-Royce Merlin 45 | |
| **Power:** 1,095kW (1,490hp) | |
| **Length:** 9.10m | |
| **Height:** 3.49m | |
| **Wingspan:** 9.80m | |
| **Wing area:** 21.45m² | |
| **Empty weight:** 2,294kg | |
| **Max take-off weight:** 3,003kg | |
| **Max speed:** 575km/h | |
| **Range:** 756km | |
| **Service ceiling:** 10,820m | |
| **Armament:** Four 7.7mm machine guns and two 20mm cannons | |

**Spitfire LF Vb EP120 (G-LFVB)**
This aircraft is one of five remaining airworthy Mk V versions in the world and was delivered to the RAF on 23 May 1942. After its decommissioning, the fighter was displayed at several RAF bases, until in 1993 it was bought and restored by the Fighter Collection from Duxford. Since 1995, the Spitfire has been flying once again. As well as a static role in the epic film Battle of Britain, the fighter was one of the stars in the film Pearl Harbor. The Fighter Collection operates another Spitfire Mk XIV MV293 (G-SPIT) with a Griffon engine.

**Spitfire Mk XIV SM832 (F-AZSJ)**
Originally a reconnaissance plane, this warbird made its first flight in March 1945. Two years later, it went to the Indian Air Force. It was only in 1978 that warbird enthusiasts brought the aircraft back to Britain and began restoration work on it. The Spitfire was converted into a fighter version, a project that was continued with a few breaks by several owners. Finally, on 22 May 1995, the restoration was accomplished: the Spitfire was once again to be seen in all its original glory. In 1997 the fighter was sold to the French warbird enthusiast Christophe Jacquard.

**Spitfire LF IXc MK732 (PH-OUQ)**
This aircraft of the Royal Netherlands Air Force memorial flight, which is based in Gilze-Rijen, is one of only a few flying Spitfires that have remained in the non-English-speaking regions of the world. From 1947, the fighter was flying for the Royal Netherlands Air Force (Koninklijke Luchtmaacht), where it was parked out in the open without any protection. In 1956, RAF soldiers just took the fighter and restored it. Then it went on a tour through Germany (visiting, amongst other places, Oldenburg, Ahlhorn and Gütersloh) and Britain. The fate of MK732 seemed to have been sealed when it increasingly became a donor of spare parts for other aircraft of the Battle of Britain Memorial Flight (BBMF). However, in 1983 the 'oldie' was handed back to the Dutch who restored it to flying condition.

**Spitfire LF IXe MK356**
This BBMF Spitfire, which was built in 1944, also participated in the film Battle of Britain, if only as a static display. In 1944, after the third crash landing of its brief operational career, the RAF put the fighter into store and has been using it as a display object ever since. Only in 1992 did the restoration of the aircraft begin; this was completed in 1997, when the fighter had its second inaugural flight.

**Spitfire PR XIX PM631**
PM631 was equipped with a Griffon engine and joined the RAF as late as 1946. Later on, the fighter was used by the aircraft manufacturer Short for meteorological purposes. In 1957, the Spitfire became part of the stock of the Historic Aircraft Flight, which was the predecessor of the BBMF. Since then, the aircraft has been flying in displays for the memorial squadron on a regular basis.

*Shortly after the war, the Royal Air Force received this Spitfire reconnaissance version that was powered by a Griffon engine; later on, it was operated by No. 2 Squadron from Wunstorf airbase in Germany. After that, the Mk XIX PS915 and the PM631 together joined the Historic Aircraft Flight of the Royal Air Force at Biggin Hill. Initially however, a career as a flight display aircraft was impossible. Instead, the aircraft was used as a 'gate guardian', adorning the gates of various RAF bases. It was only in 1987 and after a major overhaul by British Aerospace that the Spitfire was once again able to fly for the Battle of Britain Memorial Flight (BBMF).*

several other companies. On 14 May 1938, the first series-production aircraft made its inaugural flight, and as early as 29 July, No. 19 Squadron in Duxford – the airfield that is now a Mecca for warbird fans – received its first Spitfire Mk I. The versions Mk I and Mk II proved to be slightly superior to the Messerschmitt Bf 109 E, and in Britain the aircraft are regarded as the heroes of the Battle of Britain. In October 1940, Supermarine planned the development of the Mk III as the successor model, which was to be equipped with a new wing. However, Fighter Command couldn't wait for the production of this new version and demanded an intermediary solution with the more powerful Merlin 45 engine. The Mk V, which was only ever meant to be a stop-gap, was to become the most widespread version of the Spitfire, with approximately 6,500 units built. Then British fortunes in the air war changed for the worse once more when the Focke-Wulf Fw 190 appeared on the scene, prompting the Royal Air Force to demand once again a more powerful Spitfire version. Supermarine didn't disappoint its best customers and created the Mk IX. Apart from two new radiators underneath the wing that were required for cooling the Merlin 61 engine, the legendary fighter's exterior remained relatively unchanged. A total of approximately 22,000 Spitfires were built in almost 50 different versions, including reconnaissance and marine versions. Over the course of the fighter's development, both its total weight and engine power were nearly doubled and its speed increased from 585 to 730km/h. The last stage of the aircraft's development included the use of the powerful Rolls-Royce Griffon engine, and the fighter was operated by the Royal Air Force until 1951. Sadly, its designer Mitchell died in 1937 and did not live to see the triumph of his creation.

*Due to its legendary status, it is no surprise that the Spitfire is one of the most popular warbirds. There are still about 50 aircraft flying worldwide, most of them in Britain and the US. There is also a large number of Spitfires either in museums or in the process of being restored. The photograph shows a unique formation of several Spitfires and one Hurricane – a highlight at Oshkosh 1995.*

The world's oldest airworthy Spitfire is also a veteran of the Battle of Britain. The Mk IIa P7350 entered service in August 1940 and its active career ended as a museum piece on an RAF base. It was only the film Battle of Britain that made the company Spitfire Productions restore the 'oldie' in 1967. After the film was made, the aircraft joined the Battle of Britain Memorial Flight. This RAF unit, which is based in Coningsby, is in charge of the preservation of British aviation tradition.

*Legends amongst themselves: Ray Hanna and his Spitfire lead the British acrobatics team Red Arrows. The Mk IX MH434 (G-ASJV) was built by Vickers in Castle Bromwich in 1943. Shortly afterwards, in March 1945, the Spitfire was decommissioned. However, this didn't mean the end of its operative career. The warrior was bought by the Royal Netherlands Air Force in 1947 and used, amongst other places, in Indochina. Six years later, the Belgians took on the Spitfire for pilot training. After its final decommissioning in 1956, the 'oldie' found its way to Britain and in 1983, the fighter became one of the first aircraft of Ray Hanna's Old Flying Machine Company.*

The Mk Vb AB910 was built in August 1941 in Supermarine's Castle Bromwich plant. In 1947 it was used as a privately owned racing plane. After a crash landing in 1953, Vickers bought the aircraft and repaired it. In 1965, Vickers, which had been taken over by the British Aircraft Corporation, donated the 'oldie' to the BBMF.

*Above: This Mk XIV is flying for the Museum of Flying in California. The powerful Griffon engine marked the last evolutionary stage of the Spitfire.*

*In 1997, the AB910 of the BBMF made a special visit to the US for the 50th birthday celebrations of the US Air Force on Nellis Air Force Base.*

*Due to its part in many films such as* Operation Crossbow, Battle of Britain *and* A Bridge Too Far, *the Duxford-based MH434 is one of the most famous Spitfires.*

*Apart from a small museum collection, engine manufacturer Rolls-Royce also operates its own Griffon-powered Spitfire as a memorial aircraft. On 13 January 1945, the Southampton-built reconnaissance plane entered service with the RAF. Later on, it was used by Short as a test aircraft and then became a display aircraft of the Battle of Britain Memorial Flight until Rolls-Royce sold the PR XIX PS853 (G-RRGN) in September 1996.*

*When the Spitfire prototype made its inaugural flight, nobody thought that the Type 300 and its successors would be such a fantastic success.*

# The specialist

'What is the difference between a barrage balloon, a Lysander and an aircraft? The aircraft can't stand still in the air!' This common saying summarises beautifully the performance of Westland's most successful fixed-wing aircraft. It had excellent low-speed characteristics, short take-off and landing distances and good views: in brief – it was the ideal army support aircraft. Westland chose a very unusual wing shape for its monoplane. The aerodynamics specialists fitted the inner leading edge and the outer trailing edge of the wing with a negative sweep. In addition, the one-spar wing didn't have a middle section, therefore the ribs of the wing root went right through the cockpit. The fuselage was made of a steel tube construction and bore a fixed gear with a streamlined covering. The spacious cockpit lining gave the crew an excellent view. The Air Ministry's civil servants were also in favour of the design, and in June 1935 ordered two prototypes. As early as 15 June 1936, the first aircraft made its inaugural flight. Soon afterwards, an order for 169 Lysander Mk Is was placed, and the first aircraft was delivered on 15 May 1938. Later on, the first version was followed by the Mk II with the more powerful Bristol Mercury Perseus XII engine (665kW/905hp), and also the heavier version Mk III with a Bristol Mercury XX with a mere 640kW (870hp). The Lysander was used in many roles, for example as a target-tower, a marine search-and-rescue aircraft and a test aircraft. It was even briefly used as a bomber in France, but losses of 70 per cent made this role impossible. However, the Lysander became famous due to its secret night-time missions behind enemy lines. From August 1941, the supply of Resistance forces in the occupied French territories was solely down to the strange monoplane with its high-set wings. The 'Lizzies', as the aircraft were called affectionately by their pilots, also transported secret agents into enemy-held territory and rescued aircrews that had been shot down. The aircraft were mostly painted black, and were fitted with a firmly attached ladder that was used for climbing quickly into the cockpit. The aircraft's landing strips were often situated in dangerous areas and naturally no aircrew wanted to hang around any longer than was necessary to do the job. After having planned their navigation and landing site very carefully, the special aircraft would land on small fields, where agents had marked the wind direction with three torches that formed an L-shape. But the pilots always dreaded the final moments before touching down because they could never really be sure who was holding the torches down there...

## LYSANDER MK III

**Type:** Support aircraft
**Crew:** 2
**Engine:** 1 Bristol Mercury XX
**Power:** 640kW (870hp)
**Length:** 9.30m
**Height:** 4.42m
**Wingspan:** 15.25m
**Wing area:** 24.15m²
**Empty weight:** 1,977kg
**Max take-off weight:** 4,530kg
**Max speed:** 341km/h
**Range:** 965km
**Service ceiling:** 6,550m
**Armament:** One machine gun each in the gear covering and the rear cockpit (7.7mm); in addition, small bombs could be carried at demountable stump wings at the gear struts

*After the war, this 'Lizzie' was bought by a farmer who owned it until, in 1971, it joined the Strathallan Collection in Scotland. After its restoration in 1979, the Mk IIIA V9441 (G-AZWT) only made the odd flight until in 1998 its new owner, the Shuttleworth Collection, had it restored once again.*

*It only takes the Lysander about 230 metres to get airborne. Before the aircraft came to Old Warden, it was used as a target-tower by the Royal Canadian Air Force.*

In spite of nearly 1,400 Lysanders built, only a handful of them have remained worldwide. All aircraft are MK IIIs and came from Canadian stocks, the Lysander in the RAF Museum in Hendon being the only exception. Only two aircraft are in flying condition, although some restoration projects are currently being carried out. The oldest airworthy Lysander was built in 1941 and belongs to the Belgium foundation Sabena Old Timers. From 1942 until its decommissioning, the aircraft was flying for the Royal Canadian Air Force. In the 1970s, it was bought from a Canadian farm by the Brussels Army Museum. In 1982, the Sabena Old Timers began with the restoration of the Mk IIIA 2442 (OO-SOT). For this purpose, the remains of three other Canadian Lysanders were used. In August 1988, a captain of the Belgium airline Sabena piloted the Lysander's second inaugural flight. Today, the Lysander Mk III, which had been flying as G-BCWL in Duxford until 1998, can be found in Kermit Weeks' Fantasy of Flight Museum in Florida. Other complete Lysanders on display can be admired in the following museums: Imperial War Museum in Duxford (photograph), USAF Museum in Dayton, National Aviation Museum in Ottawa and Canadian Museum of Flight in Langley.

# Aviation Museums

Some of the aircraft shown in this book can be seen in the following selected museums. Other aircraft are generally only on display at airshows.

## AUSTRALIA

**Australian War Memorial**
GPO Box 345
Canberra ACT 2601
http://www.awm.gov.au

**Royal Australian Air Force Museum**
RAAF Base Williams
Point Cook Road
Point Cook, Victoria
http://www.raafmuseum.com.au

**RAAF Association Aviation Heritage Museum of Western Australia**
Bull Creek Drive
Bull Creek, Western Australia 6149
http://www.raafawa.org.au

## BELGIUM

**Musée Royal de l'Armée et d'Histoire Militaire**
Jubelpark 3
B-1000 Brussels
http://www.klm-mra.be

## CANADA

**Canada Aviation Museum**
11 Aviation Parkway
Ottawa, Ontario
K1K 4R3
http://www.aviation.nmstc.ca

**Canadian Warplane Heritage Museum**
9280 Airport Road
Mt. Hope, Ontario
L0R 1W0
http://www.warplane.com

## FINLAND

**Keskisuomen Ilmailumuseo**
Tikkakoskentie 125
FIN-41160 Tikkakoski
http://www.jiop.fi/ksimuseo

## FRANCE

**Association Jean-Baptiste Salis**
Cerny-la Ferté-Alais 91590
http://ajbs.com

**Musée de l'Air et de l'Espace**
Aéroport de Paris-Le Bourget
Boite Postale 173
93352 Le Bourget Cedex
www.mae.org

## GERMANY

**Auto- und Technik-Museum**
Obere Aue 2
74889 Sinsheim
http://www.technik-museum.de

**Deutsches Museum München**
Museumsinsel 1
80538 München
http://www.deutsches-museum.de/

**Deutsches Museum, Flugwerft Schleißheim**
Effnerstraße 18
85764 Oberschleißheim
http://www.deutsches-museum.de/zweig/werft/fws.htm

**Deutsches Technikmuseum Berlin**
Trebbiner Str. 9
10963 Berlin-Kreuzberg
http://www.dtmb.de

**Flugausstellung L.+P. Junior**
54411 Hermeskeil II
http://www.flugausstellung.de

**Luftfahrtmuseum Laatzen-Hannover**
Sammlung Günter Leonhardt
Ulmer Straße 2
30880 Laatzen
http://www.luftfahrtmuseum-hannover.de

**Luftwaffen-Museum**
Berlin-Gatow
http://www.luftwaffenmuseum.de/

**Technik Museum Speyer**
Am Technik Museum 1
67346 Speyer
http://www.technik-museum.de/

## GREAT BRITAIN

**Fleet Air Arm Museum**
Box D6, RNAS Yeovilton
Somerset BA22 8HAT
http://www.fleetairarm.com

**Imperial War Museum Duxford**
Cambridgeshire
CB2 4QR
http://www.iwm.org.uk

**Lincolnshire Aviation Heritage Centre**
East Kirkby
Lincolnshire PE23 4DE
http://www.lincsaviation.co.uk

**Royal Air Force Museum Cosford**
Shifnal
Shropshire, TF11 8UP
http://www.rafmuseum.org.uk

**Royal Air Force Museum Hendon**
Grahame Park Way
London, NW9 5LL
http://www.rafmuseum.org.uk

**Shuttleworth Collection**
Old Warden Park
Biggleswade, SG18 9EP
http://www.shuttleworth.org

## THE NETHERLANDS

**Militare Luchtvaart Museum**
Kamp van Zeist 2-4
3769 DL Soesterberg
http://www.militaireluchtvaart-museum.nl

## SWITZERLAND

**Flieger Flab Museum**
Überlandstrasse 255
CH-8600 Dübendorf
http://www.flieger-museum.com

## USA

**Air Museum – Planes of Fame**
7000 Merrill Ave
Chino, CA 91710
http://www.planesoffame.org

**American Airpower Heritage Museum**
Midland International Airport
9600 Wright Drive
Midland, Texas 79711
http://www.airpowermuseum.org

**EAA AirVenture Museum**
EAA Aviation Center
P.O. Box 3086
Oshkosh, WI 54903-3086
http://museum.eaa.org

**Evergreen Aviation Museum**
3685 NE Three Mile Lane
McMinnville, OR 97128
http://www.sprucegoose.org/

**Fantasy of Flight**
1400 Broadway Blvd.
Polk City, FL. 33868
http://www.fantasyofflight.com

**Kalamazoo Air Zoo**
3101 East Milham Road
Kalamazoo, MI 49002
http://www.airzoo.org/

**Lone Star Flight Museum**
2002 Terminal Drive
Galveston, TX 77554
http://www.lsfm.org

**Museum of Flight**
9404 E Marginal Way South
Seattle, WA 98108
http://www.museumofflight.org

**National Air and Space Museum**
7th and Independence Ave.
Washington, DC 20560
http://www.nasm.si.edu

**National Museum Of Naval Aviation**
1750 Radford Blvd.
Pensacola, FL 32508
http://www.naval-air.org

**National Warplane Museum**
17 Aviation Drive
Horseheads, NY 14845
http://www.warplane.org

**Palm Springs Air Museum**
745 North Gene Autry Trail
Palm Springs, California 92262
http://www.air-museum.org

**Pima Air and Space Museum**
6000 East Valencia Road
Tucson, AZ 85706
http://www.pimaair.org

**USAF Museum**
1100 Spaatz St.
Wright-Patterson AFB
OH 45433
http://www.wpafb.af.mil/museum/

**Vintage Flying Museum**
P.O. Box 820099
Fort Worth Texas 76182
http://www.vintageflyingmuseum.org

**Yankee Air Museum**
P.O. Box 590
Belleville, MI 48112-0590
http://www.yankeeairmuseum.org